FULL EMPLOYMENT
DEATH OF AN IDEAL, 1945-1983

BY

MICHAEL J. DISNEY

NEW MILLENNIUM
310 KENNINGTON ROAD LONDON SE11 4LD

Issued by New Millennium*
Printed and bound by B.W.D. Ltd. Northolt, Middx.
Typeset in 11pt Times New Roman
ISBN 1 85845 006 3
*An imprint of The Professional Authors' & Publishers' Association

I should like to express my appreciation to Dr Catterall,
Director of the Institute of Contemporary British
History, for advice and guidance given, and
to my wife for her help in myriad ways.

Front cover photographs:
Top L - R: J. M. Keynes, Margaret Thatcher, Professor Milton Friedman
Bottom L - R: Harold Macmillan, Harold Wilson, Lord Beveridge

To my son Nigel, 1951-1978 and my daughter Sarah, 1954-1993
Fugit hora, memoria vivit

CONTENTS

CHAPTER ONE
AN IDEAL ACCLAIMED

The 1945 Election.

There was widespread surprise, especially overseas, when on 26 July 1945, it became known that the British electorate had voted out the world-famous Winston Churchill and voted in the more self-effacing Clement Attlee to head the first Labour government in the country's history to have an overall majority.

The surprise might have been rather less had more people been aware of the findings of Mass Observation and the British Institute of Public Opinion, both of which had been registering a swing towards Labour since 1942. Moreover, a Gallup poll, published as late as 11 July 1945, had given 47% of the vote to Labour, 41% to the Conservatives and 10% to the Liberals. The result itself might have been different had the electorate been delivering a verdict on the conduct of the war, for there were many people who held Churchill in high esteem as a war-time leader but had serious doubts about him as a peace-time Prime Minister. The main concern of voters was what sort of a future awaited the millions who would soon be leaving the Forces and other war work, in particular whether there would be homes and jobs for them to go to.

Many of them had bitter memories of the poverty and distress of the pre-war years, much of it caused or aggravated by unemployment. The upheavals of war had churned things up not only on the battlefields but also in the minds of both civilians and service men and women and many of these were beginning to question whether their pre-war sufferings really had been unavoidable. It had not gone unnoticed that unemployment had virtually disappeared once the huge government expenditure on rearmament and war had begun to take effect and many were asking why, if the government could spend so much on the bad things of war, they could not do the same on the good things of peace.

Then there were the Russians. For years everyone had been told how wicked was their atheistic government and how miserable their people. For a twinkling of history such notions were banished, the murders and dispossessions forgotten. Now they were our hero-allies who had halted and hurled back the Nazi invader with a courage and resilience that only the bravest of the brave in other lands could hope to emulate. Moreover, those who purported to know about such things averred that they had been far more successful than the capitalist countries in avoiding unemployment. Did not what the Russians had achieved and the remarkable disappearance of unemployment in the capitalist countries after war had broken out prove that governments could do something about unemployment if they really wanted to?

The belief that unemployment on its pre-war scale need not return was not just a dream of simple folk who did not understand the difficulties. It also had first class intellectual backing. As far back as 1936, John Maynard Keynes had published The General Theory of Employment Interest and Money, undoubtedly one of the most influential works on economics to be published in the twentieth century, and by the end of the war its influence had penetrated deeply into both government and academic circles.

The "golden key" (or that is what it seemed to be at the time) which he proffered to the world was his concept of "aggregate demand". The classical economists, according to Keynes, had lived in a world of illusion. Where they had gone wrong was in their acceptance of "Say's Law". This "law" was propounded by the French economist, Jean Baptiste Say (1767-1832) and taught that since production by wages or profits created a similar demand, an economy was always tending towards equilibrium in which all resources of capital and labour would be fully employed. Keynes pointed out that this was patently untrue of the world of the Thirties or, if it was happening, full employment would only be achieved in the long run and, as he has so often been quoted as saying, in the long run we are all dead. The level of employment, he emphasised, depends on the aggregate demand created by investment and consumption expenditure. If in combination they failed to employ the available labour then the result is involuntary unemployment.

But there were several things which a government could do to augment demand for labour. They could unbalance the budget, they could reduce taxes, they could encourage investment by lowering interest rates and they could create jobs directly by public works and by improving what in later years became known as the infra-structure.

The Achilles heel of the Keynesian system was the impetus it gave to inflation, a phenomenon to which Keynes paid little attention in the General Theory. As his other writings showed, this was not because he failed to realise the human and economic damage it could do, but because at the time he was writing the industrial world was still suffering from the calamitous effects of the world-wide fall in prices which had started in U.S.A. and spread through the globe.

No man did more to inspire new thinking about unemployment than Maynard Keynes. As Master of King's College, Cambridge, Treasury official in two world wars and Britain's chief negotiator at the Bretton Woods (New Hampshire) Conference on the post-war monetary system, Lord Keynes, as he became in 1942, enjoyed prestige and influence in the later years of his life extending far beyond that which he had won from his General Theory.

But to the general pubic the name of Beveridge was much better known. This was mainly because of the Report on Social Insurance and Allied Services (Cmd. 6404), more often referred to as the 'Beveridge Report', published in December 1942. In the summer of the previous year Beveridge had been appointed to head a Committee of Civil Servants to enquire into the whole field of social insurance.

The Report which ensued was signed only by himself in order, as he put it, "that the departmental representatives would not be associated in any way with the views and recommendations on questions of policy which it might contain." In it he proposed that in return for a weekly contribution workers should obtain insurance against sickness, unemployment, widowhood, old age, maternity, industrial injury and funeral expenses.

The Report, arriving on the scene soon after heartening news from El Alamein and Stalingrad had begun to turn men's minds to thoughts of peace, proved a best-seller amongst White Papers. Over 600,000 copies were sold, service men and women being as avid for copies as the civilian population at home. All parties pledged themselves, if elected, to introduce a comprehensive scheme of social insurance based on this Report, although the Conservatives were rather more cautious and tentative about it all. (Beveridge himself stood and was defeated as a Liberal candidate in the 1945 election.)

In the Report, Beveridge pointed out that the insurance scheme would be impossible to implement if there was a return to mass unemployment. "The Report," he stated, "assumes, not the abolition of all unemployment, but the abolition of mass unemployment." The Plan for Social Security could itself help directly to stabilise employment by increasing the amount payable as insurance contributions in good times and reducing it in bad. But he recognised that any changes in contributions would only amount to "subsidiary measures" and that to solve the main problem of maintaining employment, other measures would be necessary.

The form which these measures might take was the theme of his book, Full Employment in a Free Society. This publication, although not in any sense an official document was, in Beveridge's own words, "a sequel to the Report on Social and Allied Services". It was also complementary to Keynes' General Theory as it outlined the practical implications for government policy if Keynes' prescription for full employment was accepted. In fact, Beveridge paid tribute in his book to the "epoch-making work" of Keynes which he said had inaugurated "a new era of economic thinking about employment and unemployment".

In order to attain the goal of full employment, Beveridge argued, there would have to be adequate outlay by government and industry, control would have to be exercised over the location of industry and there would have to be improvements in the functioning of the labour market so as to encourage the geographical and occupational mobility of workers. So long as these conditions were fulfilled, he believed that it should be possible to reduce the national unemployment rate to 3%. This was substantially less than the 8% assumed in the Plan for Social Security and not much more than one-fifth of the inter-war average of 14%. Keynes took the view that there was no harm in aiming at 3% but that he would be surprised if the government were successful in achieving it "because of the openness of the British economy to depressive influences from abroad". He would have been even more surprised had he lived to see that it would seldom be as high as 2% until the late Sixties and it would not be until the Seventies that the average level of unemployment for any full year would be in excess of 3%.

The proposals of Keynes and Beveridge inspired much of the thinking behind the Coalition Government's White Paper on Employment Policy (Cmd. 6527), published in 1944 and which enunciated the then rather novel idea that it should be "a primary aim and responsibility " of government to "maintain a high and stable level of employment". For this to come about, three conditions must be observed; total expenditure must be maintained; the level of prices and wages must be kept stable; and there must be sufficient mobility of workers between occupations and localities. The government itself could make a useful contribution to maintaining expenditure by abandoning the policy, sacrosanct in the past, of an annually balanced budget for a policy of balancing it over a longer period - in other words, by using what later came to be known as demand management or Keynesian techniques.

The White Paper was not quite the blueprint for a full employment policy of the future that it was sometimes made out to be. The language was cautious. To make the maintenance of full employment "one of the primary aims and responsibilities" of government was not the same as saying that the obligation to do so was absolute. If any of the three conditions mentioned were unfulfilled - most importantly, the one about keeping prices and wages stable - then the government of the day could argue that other economic objectives would have to take precedence.

Nevertheless, despite its understandably cautious wording, it placed a more explicit obligation on governments in the matter of full employment than had ever been done before and for many years it was accorded the nearly unanimous backing of all political parties.

But voters at that time were not juggling with future percentages: they were concerned with prospects for homes, jobs and social security in the immediate future and there is no doubt that Labour's policy, with its concentration on domestic affairs and unequivocal commitment to use the power of the State to implement that policy, was more in tune with the mood and hopes of electors than that of the Conservatives.

The main theme of the Conservatives' "Twelve Point Statement of Policy" was the need to maintain Britain as one of the great powers and to preserve and develop the Commonwealth and Empire. Not until their fifth point did full employment get a mention with the somewhat bland statement that they would follow "a determined policy for full employment and a rising standard of living".

Full employment was central to the Labour Party's manifesto, "Let us face the Future". This too contained twelve points, in the third of which they not only undertook to maintain full employment but also specified the measures by which they would do so. These included: raising production and purchasing power to the highest level by planned investment in essential industries and services; the creation of a National Investment Board to determine social priorities and the taking into public ownership of the Bank of England (a measure to which Labour policy framers at the time attached special importance) and the major industries of energy, transport and steel.

What remained vivid in people's minds was not Labour shilly-shallying in the 1931 crisis but the sequel when a National Government was elected - and everyone knew that a National Government was a Conservative government in all but name. It was this Conservative government which had left men and industries to moulder in the years of depression and the Conservatives who had devised and enforced more excruciating refinements to the hated family means test.

These memories of the recent past, coupled with the belief that, despite their protestations to the contrary, Conservatives were lukewarm about the new insurance scheme proposals cost the Conservatives many votes. With this boost behind them and capitalising on the general mood, especially amongst the young in the Forces, that the country was ripe for change, Labour, as Table 1 below shows, emerged victorious with a majority of 146 over all other parties put together.

Table 1

General Election of 5th July 1945

Party	Votes Received	Percentage of Votes	Number of MPs
Labour	11,995,152	47.8	393
Conservatives	9,988,306	39.8	213
Liberals	2,248,226	9.0	12
Others	854,294	3.4	22

It mattered little to Labour that their majority of only 8% in the popular vote was not nearly so overwhelming as their preponderance in Members of Parliament (393 Labour to 213 Conservatives) might suggest. They now regarded themselves as having a mandate to steer through Parliament the reforming legislation and economic measures by which they hoped to lay the foundations for a better Britain.

They did so, however, at a uniquely difficult time in which the euphoria of victory would be a diminishing asset and the exigencies of war a crumbling excuse for shortcomings or failure.

CHAPTER TWO
AN IDEAL ACHIEVED 1945-64

The Morrow of War - May 1945 - December 1947.

Between the wars the outstanding feature of Britain's persistent unemployment problem had been lack of demand for its industrial products, especially those of its old staple industries: coal, iron and steel, ship-building and textiles. One did not have to be a trained economist to appreciate that no unemployment need arise from this cause for some time to come. The physical damage to buildings and property, the wear and tear on capital equipment and the arrears of maintenance on road and rail systems, guaranteed that for months, perhaps years ahead there would be a demand for virtually every thing that could be produced. To this had to be added the overwhelming need to expand exports.

There was, however, a more immediate danger to full employment. Factories could only be kept going and people properly fed if the country was able to maintain imports of raw materials and food. Yet Britain's ability to pay for such imports had been dramatically reduced by the exigencies of war. It had begun the war with £600 million of gold and dollar reserves and external liabilities of £476 million; it ended the war with only £450 million in gold and dollar reserves and with external liabilities of £3,550 million. Without help from some external source - and where was it to look unless over the Atlantic? - it could not possibly pay for sufficient imports to keep the whole labour force employed.

By the end of the year, a "line of credit" had been negotiated, amounting to $3,750 million from USA and $1,250 million from Canada. Drawings on these credits could be made from mid-July 1946. Neither interest nor repayment terms were particularly harsh except in one respect, US insistence that sterling should become fully convertible within a year of the loan becoming operable, i.e. from 15 July 1947. Despite the convertibility clause there was general satisfaction that the immediate danger of mass unemployment and its concomitant hardships had been avoided.

Amid the uncertainties of the hour one thing stood out. If Britain were going to pay for its imports and fulfil its obligations to other countries in the sterling area, there would have to be a major restructuring of its industries. Manpower would be at the forefront of policy making, not in the context of avoiding high unemployment, but in the sense of increasing the size of the civilian labour force and improving its skills. An essential first step would be to accomplish efficiently the last military operation of the war, demobilisation.

It was fortunate, therefore, that the war-time Coalition government, mindful of the mistakes made in 1918-19, had drawn up careful plans for this exercise before the war ended. There was to be no disorderly skelter into civilian life. A minority (Class B) would be given early release because of their importance to industrial production or other essential activities. The order of release for the rest (Class A) would be determined partly by age, partly by length of service.

Awaiting them would be not only civilian suits and a modest gratuity but also a miscellany of other benefactions, many of them dealing with rights and opportunities connected with their future employment. Fears of immediate joblessness were forestalled by the Reinstatement in Employment Act of 1944 which required the reinstatement in their old jobs, wherever practicable, of those who had been "in the service of the Crown or in a civil defence force", whilst the Disabled Persons (Employment) Act 1944, provided what it was hoped would be a comprehensive scheme for the rehabilitation and training of disabled persons, the number of whom it was foreseen was bound to increase as fighting reached its climax. By the end of 1946, four and a half million men and women had been discharged from the forces and the number of men and women engaged on munitions reduced by over 3,500,000. In manpower terms, at least some semblance of a civilian economy had been restored.

Friction-free demobilisation and successful negotiation of an American loan gave Britain a breathing space. It did not mean that good times were just ahead - far from it. Although the physical dangers of war had passed, the hardships of peace, at least for the civilian population, were in many ways worse. Rationing and restrictions were more stringent and certainly more tiresome than in wartime. In July 1946, because of the world-wide shortage of grain, bread rationing - never imposed in the war years - was introduced and lasted for two years.

These austerities did not deter the government from embarking on the programme of nationalisation to which the Labour party had always attached such importance. Legislation nationalising the Bank of England, prime financial target, and coal, prime industrial target, was passed during 1946.

Early in 1947, people had a taste of what life would be like if it really did prove impossible to import the raw materials needed to keep the country's economy going. On this occasion the trouble was the inability, because of the snow which covered the land for nearly two months, to distribute coal supplies, so that despite draconian rationing for civilians, electricity supply was badly interrupted and many factories were unable to continue production. Unemployment soared from just over 350,000 in December to over 1,800,000 in February. By April, the total had fallen back to just below the December figure.

This temporary rise in unemployment was neither proof nor disproof of the government's ability to maintain the full employment it was pledged to over the longer term. It was, however, an economic set-back and meant that there was now less chance than ever of Britain expanding her exports sufficiently quickly to meet the demands sure to be made on her once sterling became convertible. But there was no way out of the agreement, except by proving that it was unworkable and it duly came into effect on 15 July. On 20 August $3,600 million of the combined US and Canadian loan of $5,000 million having been expended, convertibility was suspended.

The convertibility fiasco was the signal for a reappraisal of government policy and an intensification of efforts to bring Britain's financial transactions into balance. Commonwealth countries, most of whom were in the sterling area, were persuaded to reduce their dollar imports whilst life was made even more joyless for the British consumer by reductions in the meat rations, abolition of the basic petrol ration and a ban on foreign travel for pleasure. But it was recognised that even these measures would be of no avail if negated by manpower shortages in essential industries and services, a situation which might come about in three ways: if there were too few workers, if they did not have the right skills or if they had the right skills and were either not using them or using them for the wrong purpose.

There were two ways of increasing the numbers in the workforce: by recalling some of the women who had performed so magnificently in the war and by recruiting foreign workers. A special campaign was launched by the Ministry of Labour in the summer of 1947 to attract women back to work. When the campaign came to an end four months later, it was officially heralded as a success as over 30,000 women had either presented themselves for work at Ministry of Labour offices or were known to have taken up work following a direct approach to employers.

The recruitment of foreign workers was a rather more controversial affair arousing, as with Italians for coal-mining and Poles for building, some antagonism within the industry to which they were allotted. A more sympathetic welcome was given to displaced persons (later known as European Volunteer Workers, or EVWs), recruited from the refugee camps of Europe. Table 2 below shows the number of foreign workers placed in employment in Great Britain up to 31 January 1948.

Table 2

Foreign Workers Placed in Employment in Great Britain to
31 January 1948

European Volunteer Workers	Males	24,394
	Females	12,360
Polish Resettlement Corps		56,923
Polish Civilians		3,406
Italian foundry workers		331
German and Italian ex-prisoners of war placed with farmers		7,750
		105,164

Source: Ministry of Labour Gazette

One of the most serious labour problems at this time was the shortage of skilled labour. Employers' efforts to overcome this shortage were supplemented by the government in three ways. An Interrupted Apprenticeship Scheme made finance available to enable persons whose technical training had been interrupted by war service to complete their training. Similar assistance was offered in the professional field under the Further Education and Training Scheme. Thirdly, the government greatly increased the number of Government Training Centres from 17 in 1945 to 65 in 1946. Special emphasis was placed on building trade skills without which the huge programme of physical reconstruction would never be completed.

In November 1947, Hugh Dalton introduced his second budget, reducing defence expenditure and imposing further cuts in investment. A minor but unintended leak of the budget's contents on the way to the House of Commons prompted him honourably to resign, his place as Chancellor of the Exchequer being taken by Sir Stafford Cripps, champion, expositor and exemplar of the austerity he so sedulously preached.

A Better Year - 1948.

1948 proved a far better year than might have been expected. In February the Government published a White Paper (Cmd 7321) entitled "Statement on Personal Incomes, Costs and Prices", emphasising the message that Sir Stafford Cripps was purveying so vigorously to Parliament and people that consumer needs must for some time to come take third place to exports and investment. A special meeting of trade union executives in March followed the TUC lead and voted by a large majority, albeit with certain reservations, to support the policy of wage restraint for which the government were calling.

In the middle months of the year two events occurred which were to play a major part in shaping the economic and social future of Britain. These were the first drawings on Marshall Aid and the inauguration of the Welfare State.

A year earlier, in a speech at Harvard University, George Marshall, the US Secretary of State, had invited the European nations to set out their needs so that they could be jointly examined with a view to helping them fill the dollar gap which was proving such an obstacle to recovery. Thanks largely to Ernest Bevin at the Foreign Office in this country and M. Bidault of France, negotiations went through remarkably quickly and by mid-1948 proposals had been formulated, legislation approved by Congress and drawings on Marshall Aid had begun.

A Welfare State (even if the term itself is more modern) had for many years been a dream of the Labour Party; its bed-rock was to be a free health service for all and adequate financial provision for those unable to earn by reason of age, accident, illness or unemployment. To this end the government lost no time in starting the complicated and, as far as the medical profession was concerned, often acrimonious negotiations necessary before these aspirations could be turned into reality.

All was ready for a start on 5 July 1948, a date memorable in British social history as the day on which the National Health Service was inaugurated and on which both the National Insurance Act 1946 and National Assistance Act 1948, came into effect. Labour was jubilant in their conviction that they had now buried the last remnants of the Poor Law and provided for all citizens a degree of financial security which would have seemed impossible in the Thirties.

One assumption widely held was that, just as the boom of 1919 had turned into the slump of the early Twenties, so would the huge demands which had piled up during the Second World War eventually be succeeded by lower order books and shrinking demands from industry for labour. When this happened it would not only be necessary for the country to have a sound scheme of national insurance to sustain workers who had lost their jobs but also a reliable set of statistics so that governments could assess the severity and know the location of unemployment.

The new National Insurance Act introduced no new principle in the method of counting the unemployed. As before this was done by counting on one day each month the number of people who were not in employment but who were registered for work at an employment exchange or youth employment office (formerly juvenile employment bureaux). The new unemployment figures were, however, an improvement on the old because the pre-1946 Unemployment Insurance Acts had excluded non-manual workers earning more than £420 a year, teachers, nurses, private domestic servants and a few other categories. These all became insurable under the new Act, so that national, regional and local unemployment figures immediately became rather more accurate because they were now calculated on virtually the whole, instead of a portion, of the labour force.

15

Via Devaluation to General Election - Jan 1949 - Feb 1950.

Those who hoped that 1949 would also be a year of steady progress were in for a disappointment. Partly because of a mild recession in U.S.A. exports from Britain and other countries in the sterling area began to fall and the dollar deficit rose from £82 million in the first quarter of the year to £157 million in the second. The situation continued to deteriorate throughout the summer, exacerbated by mounting speculation against the pound. By September, it was clear that the pressure could no longer be contained and the pound was devalued from $4.03 to $2.80.

There is always a gap (symbolised by the J-curve) between the act of devaluation and the benefits to be derived therefrom in terms of higher exports; indeed the benefits will not be reaped at all unless the devaluing country keeps its costs down and makes sufficient resources available to match the export opportunities which its new-found competitiveness should open up.

Within weeks of devaluation, Attlee had announced cuts of £150 million on capital and £100 million on current expenditure. Financial markets in U.S.A. and U.K. reacted favourably to these measures and during the last quarter of the year gold and dollar reserves rose from £351 million at the old rate of exchange to £603 million at the new.

Labour had now been in office for four and a half years and it was no surprise, therefore, when Attlee announced that there would be a general election on 23 February.
Labour's greatest electoral assets were their achievements in social policy and their record on unemployment. Economic growth had not yet become the prize and emblem of economic success it was soon to become. It is probable that most people, equating success in economic policy with plenty of jobs, had not even heard the term. On this criterion the government could not be faulted, however much truth there might be in the comment in the Conservative manifesto, "This

is the Road", that full employment would have been likely under any government because of the world-wide demand for goods.

Between the introduction of the new Insurance Act in 1948 and the 1950 election unemployment had never risen above 400,000, or 1.8%. This was in marked contrast to what happened following the end of the First World War when unemployment shot up from 700,000 (5.8%) in December 1920 to over 1,900,000 (17.8%) in December 1921.

Had unemployment been the only issue or as dominant an issue as it was in 1945, Labour would almost certainly have been returned with a handsome majority. As it was they were vulnerable in a number of respects. Despite Harold Wilson's bonfire of controls at the Board of Trade in November 1948, enough restrictions remained to constitute a major target for Conservative campaigning. Business men were tired of being bossed about by Whitehall and ordinary people wanted to see an end to the rationing and regimentation which had been obtruding into their lives for more than a decade.

Labour's nationalisation programme - insurance, sugar-refining, cement and water supply - was an easy target for ridicule and not the sort of cause to rekindle the evangelizing zeal of 1945. Moreover, they were now fighting a Conservative party machine formidable in efficiency and dedication after nearly four years of Lord Woolton's chairmanship. There was also the Butler-inspired Industrial Charter which Conservatives hoped would convince doubters that they too did not want to return to the bad old days.

The Conservative programme and organisation were good enough to carry them tantalizingly close to victory, but as Table 3 below shows, Labour scraped home with their majority over Conservatives reduced from 180 to 17 and that over all parties (which now included only 9 Liberals) reduced from 146 to 5. The ageing Winston Churchill would have to wait a little longer. The now not-so-young Anthony Eden would have to wait a little longer.

Table 3

General Election of 23rd February 1950

Party	Votes Received	Percentage of Votes	Number of MPs
Labour	13,266,592	46.1	315
Conservatives	12,502,567	43.5	298
Liberals	2,621,548	9.1	9
Others	381,964	1.3	3

A Troubled Second Term for Labour - March 1950 - Oct 1951

At first things seemed to go well for the new government. Production rose, exports increased and the balance of payments improved. The gold and dollar reserves were now benefiting both from Britain's greater competitiveness following devaluation and by recovery in the American economy which raised U.S. purchases of wool, cocoa and other products of the sterling area primary producers. Gains in revenue from limiting food subsidies to £140 million a year and increases in petrol duty were counterbalanced by reductions in the income tax of the less well-to-do.

But on 25 June, an event happened which was to play havoc with Labour's economic policy and create serious dissensions within the party. On that day North Korean troops crossed the border into South Korea. The United Kingdom supported United Nations' condemnation of this action and agreed with the U.S.A. and other allied countries to give military backing to South Korea. With this commitment in mind and apprehensive about the implications of Middle East turmoils and general East/West tensions, the government decided on a huge rearmament programme, fixed in September 1950 at £3,600,000 and raised in January 1951 to £4,700,000 million.

The strains now being put on the economy were immense. At one and the same time the attempt was being made to increase exports, cope with the huge rearmament programme, modernise and re-equip British industry, go some way towards satisfying the increasing clamour for consumer goods and still maintain the services and benefits which the new Welfare State was expected to provide for its citizens.

The difficulties of the government were compounded by the sharp rise in the price of commodities and raw materials as the U.S.A. increased the tempo of her stockpiling. The pressures on the British economy were reflected in the labour market. Unemployment fell from 282,000 in June 1950 to 191,000 a year later, whilst unfilled vacancies in the same period rose from 384,000 to 487,000.

With this background the financing of the huge programme on which the government were embarked posed difficult budgetary problems. It fell to Hugh Gaitskell, Chancellor since October 1950, to expound these and present the government's reaction to them in his budget speech in April 1951. Revenue to be raised was £4,230 million; obstacles in the way were the sheer size of the rearmament project, the steep rise in import prices (not offset by a commensurate rise in the price of British exports) and the shortage of raw materials arising from American purchases.

The Chancellor proposed to raise the revenue required by an increase of 6d in income tax, higher duties on a variety of consumer goods and by raising tax on distributed profits. In addition, he announced that initial allowances on plant, machinery and buildings would be suspended from 1 April 1952. The object in doing so was to relieve some of the mounting pressures on industrial capacity arising from the converging demands of rearmament, exports and civilian needs. His most controversial decision so far as Labour supporters were concerned was the proposal to raise £25 million by charging National Health Service users half the price for dentures and glasses. In a budget of over £4,000 million, this was a bagatelle. But it created a major uproar in Labour ranks, culminating in the resignation of Aneurin Bevan, appointed Minister of Labour only three months earlier, Harold Wilson at the Board of Trade and John Freeman, Financial Secretary to the Treasury.

During the summer, the balance of payments continued to deteriorate and speculation against the pound intensified. The country was now being run by men who seemed, and no doubt were, very tired. Bevin had died in April and with Cripps too ill to participate in affairs and Bevan at odds with the leadership, much of the zest and cohesion of the earlier years had evaporated. Attlee decided to call an election for 25 October.

The election of 1951 was by no means a rerun of the one held twenty months earlier. Foreign affairs figured more prominently and the feeling that Labour had been inept in this field was not effaced by their attempt to depict the Conservatives as war-mongers. It was true that they still had their good record on unemployment and they plugged this very hard. "Full employment through six years of peace is the greatest of all Labour's achievements," ran their manifesto; "...it has never happened before. It has meant a revolution in the lives of people..." "Labour," they claimed, "brought new life to Scotland and Wales. The great areas of depression have gone."

The Conservatives had little to say about unemployment, merely noting in their manifesto that: "the Conservative aim is to increase our national output. Here is the surest way to keep our people fully employed."

Only a small swing was needed to return the Conservatives to power. This they achieved, as can be seen from Table 4 below, raising their percentage of votes cast from 43.5% to 48%. This was enough to win them 321 seats to Labour's 295 (even though Labour received

230,000 more votes). Liberal representation was reduced to six.

On 26 October 1951, Winston Churchill became Prime Minister once again.

Table 4

General Election of 25th October 1951

Party	Votes Received	Percentage of Votes	Number of MPs
Conservatives	13,717,538	48.0	321
Labour	13,948,605	48.8	295
Liberals	730,556	2.5	6
Others	198,969	0.7	3

Jobs Galore - Oct 1951 - Dec 1953.

The strains on the economy when the Conservatives assumed office were certainly formidable, the greatest pressures being on the metal making and metal using industries and it soon became clear that it was a physical impossibility to satisfy both civilian and military requirements at the same time. Where should the main cuts fall? Churchill gave the answer when, in a debate on Defence early in March 1952, he informed the House that "in the face of dire financial distress" the government had decided to "reduce or slow down the military defence programme on which the socialist government had embarked and to which they committed the nation".

Bevan, who had always held that the huge rearmament programme to which Britain had committed herself was beyond her capacity, had been proved right.

In other respects too the Conservatives had shown themselves ready to don Labour clothes. They were anxious to show that they were not antagonistic to the workers. By appointing Sir Walter Monckton, noted industrial peace-maker, to be his Minister of Labour, Winston Churchill had clearly signalled to the unions that what he wanted was Jaw, Jaw and not War, War.

Paradoxically, despite the strain being put on most of manufacturing industry, within a few months of taking office the government found themselves having to face the first serious unemployment problem since the war, apart from the short-lived fuel crisis of 1947. The sectors mainly affected were textiles and clothing though the boot and shoe industry and furniture were having a thin time of it.

The recession in textiles was a world-wide phenomenon due in large measure to the cessation of the stockpiling by the United States, which had boosted purchases for several months after the outbreak of the Korean war. Most employers, beset for more than half a decade by shortages of labour, preferred to put their employees on short-time rather than dismiss them and risk not being able to re-engage them when what they hoped would be a short recession was over. The number of temporarily stopped workers rose to a peak of 147,000 in May 1952; a year earlier it had been less than 7,000. After this summer peak the total fell rapidly and the end of the year amounted to only just over 30,000.

The demand for labour during 1953 was boosted not only by an expansionary budget but also by the surge forward in the building industry towards the target of 300,000 houses a year set it by the Conservative party in their 1951 manifesto. By the end of the year there were nearly 70,000 fewer unemployed and 40,000 more unfilled vacancies than there had been at the end of 1952. 1953 can well be regarded as the gateway year to the years of full employment par excellence.

Jobs Bonanza Continues - January 1954 - August 1958.

1954 ushered in a period of full employment such as modern Britain had never before experienced in peace-time. Not during a single month during the years 1954-57 did the monthly average of unemployed exceed 1.4% and on some occasions it was as low as 0.9%.

Signs, however, that there were still a few obstructions on the road to Utopia began to appear early in 1955. Imports rose both in price and volume whilst the surplus that had been achieved in the balance of payments began to evaporate. People steeled themselves for a stern budget. They need not have done so. What they got was a surprising £135 million worth of tax relief, most of it in the form of income tax reductions. It did not go unremarked that only four days before budget day Anthony Eden, who had taken over the premiership from Winston Churchill earlier in the month, had announced that there would be a general election on 26 May.

The result of the election was almost a foregone conclusion. Economic problems there might be, but they were not the sort to vex or scare the ordinary man or woman. For them the salient feature of the situation was that jobs were plentiful and pay was rising. The Conservatives could claim with confidence that they had fulfilled their undertakings about full employment. In April unfilled vacancies topped 400,000 for the first time since the Korean war boom, whilst in May unemployment fell below 1% for the first time since figures were collected under the 1946 Insurance Act.

Eden's hopes of consolidating his position with voters as well as with Parliament were realised. As Table 5 below shows, the Conservatives emerged from the election with a majority over all other parties of 58 compared with only 17 in 1951.

Table 5

General Election of 26th May 1955

Party	Votes Received	Percentage Votes	Number of MPs
Conservatives	13,286,569	49.7	344
Labour	12,404,970	46.4	277
Liberals	722,405	2.7	6
Others	346,554	1.2	3

The jobs bonanza continued under the new Parliament. In July the head-count of unemployed amounted to only 185,000. This was the lowest point since the Second World War; even at the height of the Korean war it had never fallen below 190,000.

Shortly after the July unemployment figures were published, Chancellor Butler announced a number of credit restrictions and as these measures failed to check the surge in imports and wage claims, raised both profits tax and duties on consumer goods. Still the boom continued as for six months unfilled vacancies stayed at more than 400,000. In February Harold Macmillan, Chancellor of the Exchequer since mid-December, introduced another package deal. Bank rate was raised to 5 1/2%, hire purchase controls were tightened, investment allowances were withdrawn, the public investment programme was cut and bread and milk subsidies were withdrawn.

MacMillan did not feel it necessary to follow up this powerful dose of deflation with other depressive measures and his April budget was a no change affair.

These measures did little to loosen up the labour market. After staying at 0.9% from August 1955 to January 1956, unemployment just crept up to 1.0% in February.

The obverse of the unemployment coin was a shortage of labour.

There were five main shortage categories: professional engineers and technologists; technicians; skilled manual workers, especially in engineering; machinists in textiles and clothing; men and women for more menial jobs.

The government's direct contribution to making good this shortage was minuscule. The Labour government had allowed the number of Government Training Centres to fall from their 1946 peak of 65 to only 22 whilst the Conservatives let them dwindle still further to 19 in 1957 and 13 in 1962.

This shortage of labour was the subject of continuous lamentations by employers, but only a minority did much about it. Nor did they make any bold or imaginative approach to the unions to modify their conservative and outdated stance on apprentice training.

The matter of industrial training received considerable attention early in 1956 because of the realisation that there would soon be a large bulge in school leavers entering the labour market, a consequence of the increase in births which occurred in the years immediately following the war. In June the National Joint Advisory Committee (NJAC) of the Ministry of Labour appointed a Sub-Committee under the Chairmanship of Robert Carr, Parliamentary Secretary to the Minister to examine how best this bulge of school leavers could be used in the interests both of industry and the youngsters themselves. Unfortunately, by the time the Committee reported in early 1958, the economy was in recession and it had little real effect on either the quantity or quality of training. More details of the contents and implications of the Carr Report are given elsewhere (see page 158). Within a few months of the appointment of the Carr Committee, the whole economy was plunged into temporary disarray by the Suez affair. That the upset did not prove deep or lasting was largely the work of Harold Macmillan. Having been one of the chief hawks in the plot to overthrow Abdul Nasser, Egypt's President, he became the foremost advocate of disengagement once it became clear that unless military operations ceased, the U.S.A. would block British loans from the I.M.F. and American central banks. With the announcement of a cease-fire a little more than a week after the conflict had started this blockage was removed. By drawing £200 million from the I.M.F. and arranging further credits both from I.M.F. and American banks, the government was able to stem the run on the pound which had been one of the first results of the flare-up.

Unemployment, which stood at 1.1% at the time of Suez, had risen to 1.4% in the following February but did not go above that figure for the rest of the year. The climb-down on Suez may have displeased the hawks but by preventing the imposition of financial sanctions by U.S.A., it saved an enormous number of U.K. jobs.

In political terms, the main casualty of Suez was the already ailing Prime Minister, Eden, who resigned on health grounds in January 1957, his place being taken by Harold Macmillan. The new Chancellor of the Exchequer was Peter Thorneycroft.

Recession, Recovery and Electoral Victory, Sept 1958 - Oct 1959
In September 1958, following de facto devaluation of the franc, speculators started to sell pounds in the belief that sterling would be the next in line for similar treatment. Peter Thorneycroft, the Chancellor, was convinced that the British economy would be weaker than her rivals unless she kept prices down, a sine qua non of which was to keep the money supply under control and set a limit to government expenditure.

He let it be known, when preparing estimates for the 1958 budget, that he felt it necessary to keep government expenditure constant in money terms - which, because of inflation, would mean a fall in real terms. This was something which Macmillan, with the support of most of his Cabinet, was not prepared to accept and, on 6 January 1958, Thorneycroft resigned, taking with him the two Secretaries to the Treasury, Nigel Birch and Enoch Powell.

Fortunately for the United Kingdom, external events moved in her favour during the course of the year. A fall in commodity prices, though reducing the income of (mainly Third World) producing countries, so improved the terms of trade for Britain that, despite a U.S. recession, her gold and dollar reserves rose during the year by nearly £300 million, whilst the balance of payments surplus was the largest since the war.

The other side of the picture was that industrial production fell and demand for labour shrank. The second post-war recession had arrived. There was one big difference, however, between the 1958-59 recession and that in 1952-53. In 1958-59 the slack was spread over a far wider range of industries and even at the peak, the number of temporarily stopped workers amounted to only 71,000 compared with 150,000 in 1952-53. Most of those who became unemployed in the later period had little hope of returning to their former employer.

There is always a time lag between the application and the effects of government stimuli to the economy. Despite an estimated excess in expenditure over revenue of £150 million in Heathcoat Amory's first budget, unemployment still stood at what was considered the high level of 2.1% a year later in the early spring of 1959.

The ensuing budget was the most expansionary since the pre-election budget of 1955. Ninepence was knocked off income tax, twopence off a pint of beer, purchase tax was removed from a variety of articles and investment allowances were re-introduced. By the summer of 1959, recovery was well on its way. Industrial production was soaring, the Stock Exchange was booming and the head count of unemployed which had exceeded 600,000 at its peak was hovering around the 400,000 mark. The government had now been in power for nearly four and a half years and it was no surprise when Macmillan announced that a general election would be held on 8 October.

Although the national unemployment average at 1.9% was higher than at any previous post-war election, it was neither so high in total or diffused in incidence as to constitute a serious threat to Conservative fortunes in their London and Midland strongholds. In the less fortunate regions they were more vulnerable. At the 1959 election the only region in the country with more than 2% unemployed had been Scotland with 2.1%. In 1959 three regions: North of England, Wales and Scotland, had respectively 3.1%, 3.4% and 4.0% unemployed.

Conservative failure in these regions did not threaten their prospects in the country as a whole. Most of the seats in the areas of high unemployment were unwinnable by them anyway. The general picture was one of a country being led by a remarkable leader towards another spell of prosperity and, in most areas, low unemployment. It was an additional advantage to the Conservatives that their leader was a good performer on television, now becoming the most important of all publicity media. If the country was doing so well under the present regime why change things? Almost half of those who voted (49.4%) discerned no such need. As Table 6 below shows, when all the votes had been counted, the Conservatives had increased their overall majority from 58 to 100. Labour had 19 fewer Members than before and the Liberals, though raising the votes cast for them from 2.5% to 5.9%, still had to be content with only 6 seats.

Table 6

General Election of 8th October 1959

Party	Votes Received	Percentage Votes	Number of MPs
Conservatives	13,749,830	49.4	365
Labour	12,215,538	43.8	258
Liberals	1,638,571	5.9	6
Others	255,302	0.9	1

The Birth of Neddy, November 1959 - December 1962

For almost two years after the general election the unemployment level, despite ups and downs in the general economic situation, moved slowly but consistently downwards. From the 1.9% recorded in the month of the election, it had fallen to 1.4% by the end of 1960 and by January 1961, was fractionally lower at 1.3%, where it remained for six months.

In July 1960, Selwyn Lloyd had succeeded Heathcote Amory as Chancellor of the Exchequer. In less than a year, the country was plunged into controversy over the proposal in his first budget to raise the point of exemption from surtax on earned incomes from £2,000 to £5,000.

The controversy over the budget was still raging when, in July 1961, following considerable pressure on the pound, the government introduced one of its now familiar deflationary packages. What most caught the attention of the public and angered the trade unions was the announcement of a pay pause in the public sector accompanied by the explicitly stated hope that the private sector would follow suit.

This pay pause marked the first overt if fumbling step towards an incomes policy. Thorneycroft had mooted the idea when he was Chancellor of the Exchequer a few years earlier, but because of Prime Ministerial and Cabinet opposition it had scarcely seen the light of day so far as the general public were concerned.

Now the government were intent on ensuring that the general public did know their thoughts on incomes policy and in February 1962, they produced a White Paper (Cmnd 1626) in which they put forward a "guiding light" of 2 1/2% growth in income per head per annum. The unions, still smarting under the regressive tax reliefs in the previous budget, would have none of it.

The desire for a pay pause was not the only factor which was causing the government to have second thoughts on the laissez-faire policies which had seemed to serve them so well in earlier years.

A second factor was the apparent success of the once spurned European Economic Community which Britain, in late repentance, had in August 1961 applied to join. More particularly, the government were impressed by the success which the French seemed to have made of indicative planning. The French economy, so sluggish in the early post-war years, had recently been expanding far more rapidly than the British. Much of their success was attributed to their system of Indicative Planning, the essence of which is contained in the adjectival part of its title. The government set the target in terms of growth for various sectors of industry, thereby indicating to individual companies and industries the likely level of production that could be expected of them if these targets were to be met. Companies could plan investment and expansion with greater confidence than the British, plagued by the stop-go cycle.

This was the background to the formation of Britain's National Economic Development Council (NEDC or "Neddy"). Negotiations to bring this about had been going on for some time with both sides of industry and with other interested parties. TUC agreement to participate had only been extracted at the price of excluding incomes policy from its functions although the hope of using it for this purpose had been one of Selwyn Lloyd's original aims.

At its first meeting in March 1962, Selwyn Lloyd defined the aims and objects of Neddy as he saw them, the most important of which was to achieve faster economic growth. At its second meeting, Selwyn Lloyd gave Neddy the specific task of conducting an enquiry into the implications for industry of a national growth rate of 4% per annum in the years 1961-66. Little did Selwyn Lloyd know when he addressed this meeting how short his tenure of the chair was to be. In July he was one of the victims of the "night of the long knives", when Macmillan sacked a third of his Cabinet, his place as Chancellor of the Exchequer being taken by Reginald Maudling.

There were two reasons - not everyone would regard them as justifications - for this almost unprecedented slaughter of Cabinet Ministers: loss of support for the government in the country, as evidenced by public opinion polls and by-election results; and loss of buoyancy in the economy.

For most of his Chancellorship, Selwyn Lloyd had had to deal with an economy that was overstretched but by the autumn of 1962, the government was becoming more concerned about deficient than excess demand. For the first time for three and a half years, the head count of unemployed was in excess of half a million and the seasonally adjusted rate above 2%. A succession of reflationary steps were announced. These included lifting restrictions on bank lending, the repayment of £42 million worth of post-war credits, an increase of £72 million in public investments, a reduction in purchase tax on cars and higher investment allowances for industry.

By the end of the year these measures had neither revived the economy nor dispelled the gloom. Production was still falling, the rise in wages, though moderated was still in excess of any rise in productivity whilst unemployment at 2.2% in December was at its highest level since the 1946 Insurance Act came into effect.

Recession, Recovery and Electoral Defeat, Jan 1963 - Oct 1964
Unemployment continued to rise in the New Year, the gloom and hardship which accompanied it being aggravated both psychologically and in real terms by the snow which blanketed virtually the whole country for more than six weeks. In January 186,000, in February 218,000 workers were signing on as temporarily stopped, nearly all of them because of the freeze-up. Total unemployment in the peak month of February stood at 878,000, well in excess of what it had been at its highest point in either 1952-53 or the 1958-59 recession.

There was particular concern about the situation in the worst hit regions, especially the North of England where unemployment reached 6.4% in January and 7% in February.

31

The melting of the snows enabled most of the temporarily stopped workers to return to their employment, but left unchanged the underlying situation. On unemployment grounds alone there was a good case for a reflationary budget, grounds which were reinforced by the implications of the first report from Neddy. A 4% growth rate now became a target for both government and industry, one which would not be achieved if the government were over-cautious about expansion.

It was not the disposition of Reginald Maudling, to be over-cautious and the budget which he introduced in April provided tax reliefs worth some £260 million. This boost to demand reinforced a recovery which was already under way. In the same month, the unemployment level registered its first fall (from 2.4% to 2.3%) for more than two years. At the end of the year, unemployment was down to 1.9% and the economy was bounding along at the impressive but unsustainable rate of 6% per annum. By this time, Harold Macmillan, who had never really recovered his standing in Parliament or country after his Cabinet massacre of July 1962, was no longer in the forefront of affairs, having resigned on health grounds in October 1963. his successor as Prime Minister was Sir Alec Douglas-Home, who had renounced his peerage as the fourteenth Earl of Home to enable himself to accept the post.

In the months that followed, although the balance of payments worsened considerably, the Chancellor did not halt or deflect what became known as Maudling's "dash for growth". It was not, therefore, all gloom for a government facing an election fixed for 15 October 1964. In the matter of unemployment, which meant more to the ordinary citizen than the arcana of the balance of payments, things had worked out well. By March 1964, the national average was down to 1.6%, where it remained for six months. By the month of the election, it had fallen to 1.5%. There is no doubt that the absence of any widespread concern about jobs was one of the factors which helped the Conservatives to start a little ahead in the opinion polls.

Nevertheless, Labour had several assets which they could exploit. One was Harold Wilson's reputation as an economist, which nourished the hope that Labour might be successful in ending the stop-go economic gyrations of the Conservatives. (The prestige of economists at that time stood rather higher than some years later, when the invasion of Whitehall by economists of all shapes and sizes coincided strangely with a further dip in Britain's economic performance compared with other industrialised countries.)

Another advantage to Labour was Wilson's virtuosity in front of the television cameras. Sir Alec Douglas-Home was more experienced and more confident in foreign than in domestic affairs and admitted that he was a poor performer on television. A third advantage to Labour was that they had the capacity to appeal to both realists who felt that they were the more likely of the two main parties to achieve the economic growth which all parties said was their aim and to idealists who felt that the socialist principles they professed to espouse would lead to a more equal and humane society.

These advantages enabled Labour to overhaul the Conservative lead - just. They emerged from the polls, as Table 7 shows, with a lead of a mere four over all other parties. This was not what Harold Wilson was aiming at but at least it gave him the ticket for a sojourn of unpredictable duration in 10 Downing Street.

Table 7

General Election of 15th October 1964

Party	Votes Received	Percentage Votes	Number of MPs
Labour	12,205,814	44.1	317
Conservatives	12,001,396	43.4	304
Liberals	3,092,878	11.2	9
Others	347,905	1.3	Nil

Regional Unemployment, 1945-1964.

As mentioned earlier, the outstanding feature of Britain's unemployment problem between the wars was lack of demand for the products of her former staple industries: coal, iron and steel, ship-building and textiles. In the depression of the early Thirties, the whole country was beset by high unemployment but the wounds in the areas where the declining industries were located were far more malignant than in the rest of the country.

Special Areas Acts were passed in 1934, 1936 and 1937 and two Commissioners were appointed, one for England and Wales, one for Scotland. Very little came of these appointments, despite the forceful advocacy of Sir Malcolm Stewart, Commissioner for England and Wales. It was the old story of government making a gesture but refusing to open its fist with the money to turn aspiration into reality. It is a wry reflection on how humans conduct their affairs that what came to the rescue of these areas in the end was rearmament and war.

Had there been no war the government could hardly have failed to make some response to the Barlow Report of 1940, but how adequate or imaginative is impossible to say. As it was, virtually nothing could be done about it until the war ended.

The Barlow Report got its name from Sir Montague Barlow, Chairman of a Royal Commission appointed in 1937 to examine the economic, social and strategic implications of the existing distribution of industry within the United Kingdom. Its Report was published in January 1940, its main proposal being that the government should encourage a reasonable balance of industry within each region not just within the U.K. as a whole. This would mean preventing further congestion in the populous Midlands and South and diversifying the industrial structure of the regions where unemployment was high.

These recommendations were firmly endorsed both in Beveridge's Full Employment in a Free Society and in the 1944 White Paper on Full Employment.

The gods of war, capriciously kind, wantonly cruel, had on the whole been good to these areas in the war. Most of them were sited farther away from continental airfields than the more densely populated South and Midlands and so had escaped the worst of the bombing. For strategic, as well as economic reasons, much of the country's munitions production had been concentrated there. With the declaration of peace most of this work came to a standstill, and the areas where these factories were located were able to offer premises and labour not available elsewhere.

A large number of employers were anxious to expand not only to meet the backlog of orders accumulated during the war, but also in order to have the capacity to meet what they hoped would be a sustained demand for their products once peace-time trading got into its stride.

The new Labour government were well aware that market forces alone could not in the longer term suffice to rehabilitate these areas and soon after taking office, passed the Distribution of Industry Act 1945. Under this Act, areas regarded as specially prone to unemployment were designated Development Areas. The Areas thus designated lay mainly in Central Scotland, South Wales, North East England and West Cumberland, i.e., roughly the same as the pre-war Special Areas with the addition of some major cities (Glasgow, Dundee, Cardiff, Swansea and Newcastle).
The Board of Trade was made responsible for implementing the Act which empowered the government to build factories, provide basic services, reclaim derelict land and make loans to individual firms. The Barlow Commission had attached great importance to supplementing inducements to expand and diversify in the areas of high unemployment with measures to restrict expansion in areas of low unemployment.

The government had two instruments it could use for this purpose. One, the system of building licences, was a survivor from wartime controls, not finally abolished until 1954. The other derived from powers given to the government under the Town and Country Planning Act of 1947 to grant or refuse an industrial development certificate to an employer wishing to expand or start a new project.

The building licence system was simplicity itself for the government, though condemned by those who felt that the best way ahead was to allow employers to open up or expand when and where the prospects of profit were best. If a licence was refused an employer had three choices. He could move into existing premises, if he could find any suitable, he could move to an area for which the government would be willing to issue a licence or he could abandon his project altogether.

Under the Town and Country Planning Act, the Board of Trade were empowered to issue industrial development certificates for projects over 5,000 square feet if they considered them to be consistent with the proper distribution of industry. (For projects of 5,000 square feet or less no such certificate was needed.) Even this was not the last hurdle for an employer: he still had to get local planning permission before he could go ahead. Possession of an Industrial Development Certificate (I.D.C.) was no guarantee that planning permission would be granted; without an I.D.C. the application would not even be considered.

Another Distribution of Industry Act was passed in 1950, the main provision of which was to make additions to the financial inducements which governments could offer to firms or people moving to Development Areas.

In view of the commitment of all parties to full employment and the importance which future voters would obviously attach to success or failure in this matter, no political party could have left things to chance. Legislation to promote a better distribution of industry (and jobs) was a political if not an economic necessity. Nevertheless, the best

36

promoter of jobs in the Development Areas has always been prosperity in the country as a whole and in terms of jobs, the whole of labour's 1945-51 term of office were years of prosperity.

However, two points of significance for the future emerged in this period. The first was the relative and absolute decline in approvals for new buildings in the Development Areas. In 1945-47, 51.3% of square footage approved lay in the Development Areas, in 1948-51 only 19.4%. Employers seemed reconciled to settling in these areas when there was no alternative, but once premises and to a lesser extent labour became available in other parts of the country, they left no doubt that their preference was for what to most of them were their home regions of the Midlands and the South.

The other significant point was that despite the passage of various Acts of Parliament to give these areas preferential treatment, the gap between the richer and poorer regions remained wide and augured ill for any future in which the general level of unemployment was high. The 3.7% recorded in Wales and 3.1% recorded in Scotland during Labour's last full year of office, compares well with what was recorded in the 1930s and what it would again climb to in the late Seventies and Eighties, but badly with the 0.3% in East and 0.5% in West Midlands.

Industrial development certificate policy was also tightened up in order to end the practice whereby employers in large conurbations were evading the spirit of previous Acts by converting warehouses or other large buildings into factories. In future, they would only be able to do so if they had been granted an I.D.C. for this purpose.

Although the Conservatives entered office when the economy was about to run into the post-Korean textile crisis, the resulting increase in unemployment was short-lived and mostly took the form of employees being put on short time rather than being dismissed. By early 1953, the crisis was over and the economy was clearly on the upturn again. The years 1954-57 were the years of lowest unemployment ever recorded in peacetime and all regions shared to some extent in the jobs bonanza which ensued.

During this period the government allowed the Distribution of Industry legislation to remain on the statute book, but made little use of it. They could argue convincingly that there was no need to as all regions were enjoying full employment without any help from the government.

Things began to change in the 1958-59 recession. In Wales and Scotland and, to a lesser extent, North and North West England, the employment market began to crumble. By the end of 1958, unemployment in Wales and Scotland - for the first time since the war - exceeded 4% and in the other two regions exceeded 3%.

The government undertook to apply the location of industry policy more rigorously and, in particular, to curb industrial expansion in the larger cities such as London and Birmingham. They also introduced the Distribution of Industry (Industrial Finance) Act of 1958, to supplement but not replace earlier legislation. This Act empowered the government to make grants or loans to any businesses (not just manufacturing) in any area where the Board of Trade was satisfied that a high rate of unemployment existed or was likely to come about.

By the end of 1959 most parts of the country had made a good recovery and national unemployment was down to under 2%. Not so in Scotland, North of England and Wales, where it was respectively 4.3%, 3.4% and 3%. Shipbuilding, so long bolstered by the backlog of orders after the war, was now in long-term decline, whilst coal, so desperately short in the late forties and early fifties, was having to cope with a buyers' market.

The government's response was the Local Employment Act, 1960. This Act repealed previous legislation and introduced the new concept of Development Districts. These were based on employment exchange areas, the object being, in the words of the legislation itself, "to promote employment in localities in England, Scotland and Wales, where high and persistent unemployment exists or is threatened". The criterion for Development District status was actual or imminent unemployment of 4% or more.

Powers to make grants contained in earlier legislation were repeated in the 1960 Act with the important addition that grants would now be available to firms wanting to build their own factories in Development Districts. They would no longer have to accept one of the government's advance factories or nothing at all.

In the 1962-63 recession, as had happened in 1958-59, unemployment in the three worst hit regions rose well above that in the rest of the country. The situation was particularly bad in the North of England where unemployment reached 7% in February 1963. Although the government appointed Lord Hailsham as Minister with Special Responsibilities for the North East and despatched him (cloth-capped and ebullient) to the area, nobody proclaimed or expected a quick cure to be forthcoming. A few months later, Edward Heath was designated Secretary of State for Industry, Trade and Regional Development, recognition that the malaise in the depressed parts of the country was likely to persist even when the rest of the country had put recession behind it.

The government's response was more budget concessions, more legislation and more discussion, written and verbal. The 1963 budget allowed firms in Development Districts to depreciate investment in plant and machinery at any rate they chose. In effect this was as good as an interest free loan for firms wishing to postpone payment of their tax liabilities. The Local Employment Act 1963, introduced a standard grant of 10% for new plant and machinery, something which had not been available before, whilst the building grant made available under the 1960 Act was now set at a standard rate of 25%.

Ample material for debate and discussion were provided by two White Papers and two NEDC publications, all issued during 1963. The

White Paper on Central Scotland (Cmnd 2188) and that on North East England (Cmnd 2206), both recommended the establishment of growth areas or zones on which financial aid and infra-structural improvements should be concentrated. The hope was that the improved economic and social well-being of these areas would ripple into neighbouring areas, thereby extending the terrain which would benefit.

In the same year, two NEDC publications, Growth of the United Kingdom Economy to 1966 and Conditions Favourable to Faster Growth, pointed out that the high unemployment and low activity rates in these regions reflected a considerable labour reserve, which could be very useful in promoting economic growth. The existence of unused labour in these areas was also, as will be seen, a cardinal feature of the ill-fated National Plan devised by the next Labour government.

CHAPTER THREE
AN IDEAL UNDERMINED, Oct 1964 - Feb 1974

Increasing their Majority, Oct 1964 - April 1966.

By the time Labour came into office in 1964, the country had enjoyed 25 years of full employment and most people now assumed this to be the norm. The old fears had been exorcised, or so it was thought.

Yet unemployment was still a tricky subject for politicians to handle and the government were well aware that if they were to achieve the economic growth which was one of their prime objectives, there would have to be a considerable redeployment of labour. This could not be done without a certain number of people losing their jobs in the process. Unfortunately, declining industries do not normally shed their labour in the locations or with the skills that the new and expanding industries require. It was politically necessary, therefore, irrespective of humane considerations, to ensure that the operation be conducted as painlessly as possible.

Between taking office in 1964 and facing the electorate again in 1966, two pieces of legislation were passed and a third promised designed to mitigate the consequences of unemployment. These were a scheme for Redundancy Payments, provision for unemployment (and sickness) benefits to be related to earnings and the creation of a Ministry of Social Security.

A Redundancy Payments Act was passed in the summer of 1965 and became operative in December of that year. This Act provided that any person over 18 who became redundant after being with an employer for two years or more, should be entitled to a lump sum in severance pay. The amount depended on the length of service plus age, and would be met partly from government funds and partly by employers themselves.

A Bill to introduce earnings related benefits (already part of the social security provision in a number of other countries) received the Royal Assent shortly before the 1966 election and came into force in the following October. Initially, payment was to be equivalent to a third of a claimant's weekly earnings between £9 and £13 over the last completed tax year. Needless to say, the amounts payable both as Redundancy Payments and earnings-related benefit, were revised sharply upwards in money terms in the years of inflation which were not far ahead.

In August 1966, the Ministry of Pensions and National Insurance was merged with the National Assistance Board to form a new Ministry of Social Security, just as Beveridge had recommended more than twenty years earlier. As soon as practicalities allowed claimants for supplementary benefit (the new name for national assistance) and for national insurance would be dealt with in the same premises. These new arrangements and the sharp rise in unemployment in later years, led to a significant increase in the numbers claiming supplementary benefit, the figures rising from 172,000 in 1966 to more than half a million in 1975.

It was also the government's stated intention to improve the supply side of the labour market by giving more people better training than before. A start had been made by the Conservative government which had passed an Industrial Training Act in March 1964. It was left to the Labour government to put it into practice. Its contents and the changed Conservative attitude to its levy/grant provisions are given later in this book (see p 161).

Though they had acceded to power, Labour's room to manoeuvre was limited by two constraints. The first was the narrowness of their majority both in Parliament and the country (barely 200,000 out of more than 27 million votes cast). The second was the decision by the Prime Minister to rule out devaluation as a policy option, even though many MPs and most economists considered this self-imposed encumbrance to be a mistake.

The strategy of the government was to hang on until circumstances were sufficiently favourable for them to call an election with every chance of winning a clear majority. To do this they had to somehow gain more of the middle ground without alienating their own supporters and without provoking the sort of crisis which would lead to an unstoppable run on sterling.

Harold Wilson had promised the country to "harness the white heat of the technological revolution" to British industry. In pursuit of this aim, two new entities on the political scene were created: a Ministry of Technology and a Department of Economic Affairs (DEA). The role of the first was to encourage British industry to use the best of modern technology and, in particular, to keep up with other countries in applying the wonders of computers to manufacturing and other processes.

It was intended that the DEA should act as a counterpoise to the Treasury, who were regarded by the Labour movement in general as being by tradition and conviction, unsympathetic to the type of planning which they believed held the key to economic progress. Though no formal demarcation lines were drawn up, the general idea was that the DEA should concentrate on the real economy and the long term, whilst the Treasury exercised its traditional control over finance and the short term.

Some idea of the sort of difficulties in store for the government was indicated by the reaction to the budget introduced by James Callaghan, the new Chancellor of the Exchequer, on 11 November. On the expenditure side, he announced increases in social security payments, an end to the earnings rule on widows' pensions and abolition of charges for National Health Service prescriptions. On the revenue side, there were to be increases in national insurance contributions and rises of 6d a gallon on petrol and 6d also on the standard rate of income tax. He gave notice that he would be introducing a capital gains tax and would replace existing income and profits tax by a Corporation Tax. On a strict accountancy base, in a full year revenue would be increased rather more than expenditure.

The City and foreign financiers, always more censorious of a Labour than a Conservative government, reacted as if it had been the budget of a wanton. Any government, they seemed to feel, which was prepared to spend so much on "welfare" when there were so many other urgent problems to be solved, must be irresponsible. Within days of the publication of the budget, a run on sterling started which was not stemmed by the raising of the Bank Rate from 5% to 7%. Pressure was only eased after the Bank of England, under strong pressure from Wilson himself, succeeded in raising a credit of £3 billion from the Central Bank of U.S.A. and EEC countries, to be followed a few weeks later by a "stand-by" arrangement with the IMF by which the United Kingdom was enabled to draw up to $1,000 million within the coming twelve months.

These measures eased but did not remove the pressures on sterling and fears of another run on the pound determined the contents of the budget in April 1965, in which £250 million was taken out of the economy. This was achieved mainly by increased duties on drink, tobacco and other consumer goods and by reductions in defence expenditure, notably the cancellation of the TSR2 plane, to the chagrin of the aircraft industry and the military.

Naturally the Labour government, which had gained office on a ticket of expansion and an end to stop-go found it unpalatable to foist such measures on the country. But the action was not so drastic as seriously to dent their confidence that, given a little more time, they would win acclaim - and another general election - by generating the economic growth which had eluded the Conservatives in their latter years.

The framework under which this growth was to be achieved was the National Plan which was trumpeted to the nation in September 1965. It all ended in such fiasco, mauled beyond recovery by the July 1966 economy measures, that it is difficult now to recapture the high hopes that were embedded in it in the early months of the Labour government.

The Plan set out a growth target of 25% increase in national output by 1970. This would mean an increase of 3.8% a year, not very different from the 4% growth rate postulated by Neddy two and a half years earlier in Growth of the UK Economy to 1966. Amongst the blessings which it would confer on the country, was the creation of 800,000 new jobs, a high proportion of them to accrue in the Development Areas. Difficulties might arise from shortage of labour in some parts of the country, but at least there would be new hope in the areas where the Conservative government's full employment policies had been least successful.

Meanwhile government restrictive measures had not had dire effects either on employment prospects or on the general standard of living. The 1.5% level of unemployment when Labour came to power had fallen to 1.3% in January 1965 and throughout the year never exceeded 1.4%. In January 1966, for the first time for nine years, it was down to 1.2%. Nor had the general public done badly as consumers. The rise in earnings during 1965 (7.3%) was well ahead of the rise in prices (4.8%).

However unnerving to the politician contemplating the balance of payments and the weakness of sterling, it could not be denied that high earnings and low unemployment furnished a propitious background for any government looking to go to the country. A by-election at Hull at the end of January showed a swing of 4 1/2% to Labour. It was no surprise, therefore, when at the end of the following month, Wilson announced that polling day would be 31 March.

Labour's election manifesto slogan "You Know Labour Government Works" sums up the theme in which they went to the country. Were Wilson and his team trustworthy and capable enough to be granted a further term of office? This, rather than any specific issue was what the main electoral battle was about.

Unemployment was a very ancillary item. With the national average still at only 1.2% during the election campaign, the Conservatives could hardly criticise Labour for any lapses in this field of endeavour, whilst in view of the Conservatives' remarkable record from 1951 to 1964, Labour could not plausibly resurrect the old parrot cry that the Conservatives were the party of unemployment. It is not surprising, therefore, that in David Butler's analysis of election addresses, only 8% of Conservatives and 16% of Labour candidates, referred to unemployment. In both instances, this was the smallest number since Butler and his teams first covered the elections in 1951.

When the votes had been counted, as Table 8 shows, Labour emerged with a lead of 97 over all other parties.

Table 8

General election of 31 March 1966

Party	Votes Received	Percentage Votes	Number of MPs
Labour	13,064,951	48.0	363
Conservatives	11,918,433	41.9	252
Liberals	2,327,533	8.5	12
SNP	128,474	0.5	Nil
Plaid Cymru	61,071	0.2	Nil
Others	263,144	0.9	Nil

Deflation and Devaluation, April 1966 - Nov 1967

Early in 1966 the trade gap widened once again, but the distractions of electioneering prevented the government from doing (or saying) much about it. Many people now, Cabinet Ministers amongst them, felt that once the election was over, the government's strong political and weak economic predicament presented a unique opportunity to devalue the pound. They could face up to the short-term disadvantages with relative impunity and reap the long-term benefits well before another election was due. It was no go. Wilson remained as adamant as ever, as he assembled his new Cabinet on April the first.

The alternative to devaluation was another dose of deflation and it would have to be a fairly severe one if a new run on the pound was to be avoided. But there was a snag. Callaghan, during the election campaign, had stated that he "did not foresee the need for increases in taxation". How was he to get round this one? The answer came on 2 May when he unveiled, in his budget speech, a completely new formula for revenue raising, one which, he also claimed, would encourage the movement of labour out of low export potential service to high export potential manufacturing industries. Under this Selective Employment Tax (SET), employers would have to pay a weekly tax in respect of each of their employees.

Refunds, or "premiums" as they were called, would be made some weeks later to employers in manufacturing industry but not to employers in service industries or construction.

More will be said about SET a little later (see page 150). Here it is sufficient to note one major snag about it. It would not be in operation until September, whilst what was wanted according to the government's critics, was something which would have more immediate effect.

Long before the first pound of SET became payable, the government were caught up in the most damaging industrial dispute they had yet had to face. A fortnight after the budget, British seamen (for the first time for 50 years) went on strike in support of a wage claim well above the 3 1/2% norm agreed between the government and a reluctant TUC earlier in the year. It was more than six weeks before they went back to work, having gained not everything they had asked for, but at least a settlement which would eventually mean a rise in take-home pay of around 17%.

The pressures on the pound which inevitably followed the outbreak of the strike, increased the number and strengthened the arguments of the advocates of devaluation. George Brown brought the (previously "unmentionable") matter up in Cabinet, but his advocacy was firmly rejected by the Prime Minister with no effective dissent from the rest of the Cabinet.

One option that was not open to the government was to leave things as they were and Wilson let the House know that he would be revealing the government's intentions on 20 July. Few people foresaw how Draconian those measures would be.

The duty on consumer goods was raised by 10%, the public investment programme was cut by £150 million (housing, schools and hospitals being exempted), the foreign travel allowance was limited to £50 as from the autumn and economies to yield £100 million were made in civil and military expenditure overseas. The total effect of these measures was intended to reduce demand by £500 million in a full year.

But what created the greatest sensation amongst Wilson's audience, both inside and outside Parliament, was his announcement that there was to be a six-month standstill on wage, salary and price increases, to be followed by a period of "severe restraint".

The stop-go alternations of the later years of Conservative rule had accustomed people to periodic cutbacks, but they had never been subjected to a battering of quite such severity.

It was all very galling to Labour supporters, especially those on the left of the party who were not slow to voice their indignation and dismay. Only a week before, Frank Cousins (who had resigned from the Cabinet earlier in the month because he thought their incomes policy was "meaningless and wrong") had joined together with 49 other Labour MPs in calling for the rejection of the original, and milder, Prices and Incomes Bill. Now they were faced with something far more severe.

There was naturally concern, not confined to the left wing of the Labour party, about the effect all this might have on jobs, especially in view of Wilson's references to a labour "shake-out" in his 20 July speech. "What is needed," he had said, "is a shake-out which will release the nation's manpower, skilled and unskilled, and lead to a more purposive use of labour for the sake of increasing exports and giving effect to other national priorities. This redeployment can be achieved only by cuts in the present inflated demand, both in the public and the private sectors. Not until we can get this redeployment through an attack on the problem of demand, can we confidently expect the growth in industrial production which is needed to realise our economic and social policies."

Answering questions which followed his statement, the Prime Minister said that the measures he had outlined were expected to raise the average level of unemployment throughout the country: "from about 1 1/2% to between 1 1/2 and 2%, after all the reabsorption and redeployment and measures for regional distribution." This level he did not think the House would find unacceptable. What the government did intend to avoid was a situation: "where the level of unemployment was o.7% in half of the country and 12% in other areas."

What he was, in effect, asking the House to do was to accept an unemployment level of half a million or so, just the sort of level that would have been predictable had Prime Minister Macmillan and his Cabinet agreed to the reductions in expenditure proposed by Peter Thorneycroft in January 1958. Nor was it far off the level which Professor Paish and his followers had recently been advocating and condemned for advocating by the devotees of full employment.

It would be exaggerating to argue that acceptance of this sort of level of unemployment meant the abandonment of the full employment policy pursued by all governments since the war. But it does mark the watershed between the era in which full employment considerations were paramount and the era when it was one of several economic objectives.

These July measures had implications beyond the employment field, the most serious of them being the slow-down in economic growth which was bound to ensue. It also presaged the death, before it was even one year old, of the National Plan, and the restoration of the Treasury to its old primacy. George Brown was quick to react, resigning on 20 July, and withdrawing his resignation following the pressure of friends on the following day. Although he withdrew his resignation, he was not reconciled to the part he would have to play in a now subordinate DEA. Early in August, he got himself appointed Secretary of State for Foreign Affairs and in March 1968 resigned from the Cabinet altogether.

The Labour government could carry on without the support of individuals, however powerful, but would find it hard to do so without the support of the TUC.

Wilson lost no time in taking his case to the trade unions. On 26 July, he held discussions with the executive committee of the TUC and on the following day, the General Council gave him support by the far from overwhelming majority of 20 votes to 12, a decision endorsed by an even narrower majority (4,936,000 to 3,814,000) at the TUC Annual Conference in September.

There was also plenty of concern about the government's policy amongst back bench MPs and within the Labour party throughout the country. Reflecting these feelings, the Labour Party Conference at Brighton, like the TUC, gave the government only lukewarm support by the not very heartening margin of 3,836,000 to 2,515,000. This general backing for the government did not inhibit the floor of the Conference from passing resolutions critical of certain aspects of government policy, notably their failure to prevent the rise in unemployment.

By the time the Conference assembled in October, the head count of unemployed had risen from a total of 264,000 in July to 340,000 and the percentage rate from 1.3 to 1.6. Particularly concerned at this rise was the Transport and General Workers Union, whose motion it was that called on the government "in view of the sharp growth in unemployment, particularly in the motor industry, to prevent employers from discharging workers without consultations and negotiations with the unions and to insist on short-term working or other means as an alternative to dismissals".

An indication of the feelings of workers in that industry received more publicity when proceedings at the Conference were interrupted by a demonstration of unemployed car workers who had marched to Brighton to draw attention to their plight.

As so often in the past, the motor industry had suffered more than most from the changes in hire purchase regulations. The numbers laid off for all or part of the week had risen from 8,000 in August to 78,000 in October. Much of the short-term working was concentrated in the British Motor Corporation, which announced in September that they would be dismissing 12,000 production workers in November. A shock was also delivered to a section of the workforce unfamiliar with the trauma of redundancies when ICI announced that 1,050 production workers in their nylon plant would have to be dismissed.

In January 1967, the head count of unemployed topped the 600,000 mark. This level had only been reached twice before since the 1946 Insurance Act came into effect. This had happened in the winters of 1958-59 and of 1962-63 and on both these occasions, rising unemployment had been the signal for vigorous reflation. It was a sign of the new times and changed priorities that there was no hint of such reaction on this occasion.

The government could at least claim by early 1967 that their deflationary measures, however unfortunate in terms of

51

unemployment, were having favourable effects on the balance of payments. A mild optimism ensued, enhanced by a fall in the inflation rate to under 4%. By the end of March, all short-term debt to central banks had been repaid and Bank Rate lowered from 7% to 6%.

Callaghan, when presenting his neutral budget of 1967, spoke in terms of 3% growth rate in the economy - not quite up to National Plan or Neddy aspirations, but well above what seemed likely at the time of the 20 July package. An old naval hand himself, he summed up the government's assessment of the situation as follows: "We are back on course. The ship is picking up speed. The economy is moving. Every seaman knows the command at such a time, 'steady as she goes'."

The optimism of early 1967 did not long survive the budget. Clouds first began to gather in May when bad trade figures were received. The trade figures were of particular interest at that time because Britain had just made formal application to join the European Economic Community and the belief was widespread that if the application were successful, additional strain, in the short run at any rate, would be placed on the balance of payments. Would Britain, in those circumstances, be able to maintain the pound at its present value? Very few foreigners thought she would and once again the pressures mounted.

Sterling was further weakened when, following the outbreak of the Six Days War in the Middle East in June, Arab oil producers imposed an embargo (which in fact proved only to be temporary) on oil exports to both UK and USA. Nor did it help things from the British point of view, when in July the OECD published a report which emphasised how small Britain's currency reserves were in proportion to her liabilities.

Of more immediate concern to many Labour supporters was the continued high level of unemployment. Although it had levelled off by the summer, the head count was still in excess of half a million and the seasonally adjusted average, for the first time for over four

52

years, stood at 2%.

Neither supporters nor opponents of the government were prepared to accept this level of unemployment as tolerable. There was particular concern about the number of school-leavers who had not found work by the middle of September - 65,700 or 24,000 more than at that time in the previous year.

The TUC at their Conference the same month, had passed a resolution deploring the government's "use of deflationary measures to manage the economy which involves the creation of a pool of unemployment."

Speaking to the Labour Party Conference in October, Wilson tried to reassure his audience that he was not asking them to turn their backs on the policy of full employment. "We reject," he said, "as an instrument of policy the creation of a permanent pool, as they call it, of unemployment."; adding, "Our aim, our whole policy, is to secure full employment and to secure it on a permanent basis."

But MPs were still very sensitive on the subject, as was well illustrated by a row which blew up within the party only a few weeks later, and in which a large number of them directed their wrath on Callaghan. The genesis of the row was a speech to the Anglo-American Chamber of Commerce delivered by Sir Leslie O'Brien, Governor of the Bank of England, whose words were taken (and probably intended) to mean that Britain should run her economy at a rather higher level of unemployment. His claim was that: "Labour now accepted that it was impossible to manage a large industrial economy with the very small margin of unused manpower and resources that characterised the British economy in the 1940s and 1950s," and that "we must have a somewhat larger margin of unused capacity than the one we used to try and keep."

On 7 November, in the debate on the amendment to the address, Callaghan said that the government was not concerned with the total level of unemployment, but rather with its distribution. "What I will not advise the Labour Party or anyone else to get back to is the situation when there were eight vacancies in the Midlands for every skilled man. At the present time, there is something like a vacancy for every unemployed man. The real problem of how we increase the resources of this country is, to my mind, basically a question of the distribution of resources between the regions, like Wales, Scotland, the North and the rest of the country." "The government's policy," he added, was directed to ensuring a higher level of use of resources in those regions "without overwhelming London, the South East and the Midlands, as we have done in the past...That is why I have resisted the general reflation in present circumstances."

A few days later, 70 MPs (by no means all of them left-wingers), put down and signed a motion, "deploring" and "repudiating" the approval given by Callaghan in his speech of 7 November to O'Brien's "advocacy of a permanent pool of unemployed". Callaghan's statement had not, in fact, differed much in substance from what Wilson had said in July 1966. But since then, a new nervousness about jobs had spread throughout the Labour Party and many MPs were determined that a Labour government should not accept as normalcy a rate of unemployment markedly higher than that at which the Conservatives had managed to run the economy.

By the time the 70 MPs had signed their critical motion, Callaghan's mind was very much on other things. During October and early November, the pressures on the pound which had been building up during the summer intensified, the confidence of sterling holders being further undermined by dock strikes in London and Liverpool, which started in September and dragged on for two months. Devaluation, so long deferred, was seen even by Wilson himself to be inevitable. At 9.30pm on the night of Saturday 16 November, it was announced that the pound had been devalued from $2.80 to $2.40.

At last the deed was done. Why was it not done earlier, either when Labour first assumed office or in the even more politically favourable aftermath of the 1966 election victory? No unequivocal answer has ever been forthcoming. It is reasonable to assume, however, that Wilson felt that his Party's, and his own, prestige were very much at stake. Some stigma still attached to Labour as the party in power when Britain went off the gold standard in 1931 and when she devalued in 1949. Wilson's aim in the 1960s was that Labour should displace the Conservatives as the natural party of government. It would not help the cause if they were to be associated with yet a third currency debacle.

Wilson himself blamed much of the chronic weakness of the pound not only on the shortcomings of the British economy but on speculation by those at home and abroad who were "more concerned with making money than with earning money". In his Personal Record of the years 1964-70, he emphasised that by delaying devaluation for three years, "the whole world recognised that there was no alternative", and for these reasons: "they backed us wholeheartedly, very few countries devaluing at the same time."

It is more likely that the verdict of history will be that the prolonged adherence to an unrealistic pound/dollar rate only increased the magnitude, painfulness and duration of the adjustment that had eventually to be made.

In Balance but Out of Office, Nov 1967 - June 1970
The story of the eighteen months after devaluation was one of successive measures of deflation, starting with the Prime Minister's announcement of a medley of cuts on the Monday following devaluation and culminating in Roy Jenkins' neutral budget of April 1969.

Looking back on those years in the knowledge of how unemployment soared in the Seventies and Eighties, it may seem surprising that no such rise took place during this Labour government's long deflation. At the time devaluation was announced, in November 1967, the unemployment rate was 2.3%; when Jenkins presented his 1969 budget, it was 2.2%. During all the intervening months, it had remained stable, never rising above 2.5% and never falling below 2.1%.

There were several reasons why it remained so static. One was the high level of public expenditure, both military and civilian. The UK was spending far more on defence than her European neighbours and many of the reductions proposed in this sphere, for example, withdrawal of troops from East of Suez, would have no immediate effect. Similarly, in civilian matters postponement of capital expenditure on infra-structure and other projects had more relevance to future than current labour demands.

Pertinent too was the government's social policy which by cushioning poorer people from the most severe effects of the cut-backs, helped to maintain the income of a section of the population which would spend most of it. (In Keynesian terms, who "had a high propensity to consume.") The introduction of statutory redundancy payments and earnings-related benefits, coupled with rises in the value of retirement, unemployment and other pensions, also helped to keep up the demands for goods and services, despite the general deflation. There was also in the last year or so of the Labour government the jump in earnings which followed the lifting of wage and salary controls.

A more disturbing reason why unemployment remained low was that British industry was still seriously overmanned compared with her main industrial rivals. British industry remained labour intensive not just because of trade union opposition to modernisation, though this was a factor, but also because the economic climate was discouraging to investment in labour-saving machinery. Britain was to pay a high price for this backwardness in the Seventies and Eighties, when she became the pace setter in the surge in unemployment which afflicted almost all industrial countries.

Perhaps the real significance of what happened in the labour market in the years following devaluation, was not the stability of the unemployment figures but the equanimity with which stability at over half a million was accepted by politicians, the media and the general public.

Concern about unemployment might have got more of a hearing if it had not been for the acrimony from 1966 onwards, created by the government's incomes policy and the even greater furore which arose from their attempt to "reform the unions".

The six months standstill on wage and salary increases announced by Harold Wilson in July 1966 had been extended by another six months and followed by a "zero norm" lasting until mid-1968. For the following year a norm of 3% was fixed. From mid-1969, the lid was off as all wage negotiators scrambled to make up for lost time and lost income. Rancour on this score between government and unions was for the moment over, but the government was getting increasingly exasperated at the number and chaotic nature of strikes in industry and the desire which they now evinced to "reform the unions" was very understandable.

In the international league table of days lost by strikes, the United Kingdom came about in the middle, although, as Table 9 shows, such days had been rising rather alarmingly since the late Sixties.

Table 9

Year	Number of Working Days Lost in Strikes (in thousands)
1965	2,925
1966	2,398
1967	2,787
1968	4,690
1969	6,846
1970	10,980
1971	13,551
1972	23,909
1973	7,197

Source: Department of Employment Gazette.

What exacerbated the situation here was that so many of the strikes were unofficial or wild cat, the unions often having little more influence than the employers over their members. It was not so much the loss of production that was damaging; this could be made good once the strike was over, albeit often at the cost of expensive overtime. The real harm was to be measured in the diversion of managerial time, the postponement of investment, the discouragement to innovation and the damage done to Britain's reputation overseas for punctual and reliable delivery.

In February 1965, the government had appointed a Royal Commission on Trade Unions and Employers' Associations under the chairmanship of Lord Donovan. Their report, delivered three years later, was painstaking and penetrating in analysis, but short in terms of positive recommendations.

There was something in Iain McLeod's gibe that it was a "blueprint for inaction". But inaction was not what the public wanted or what was intended by Barbara Castle, Secretary of State, since April 1968, of the Department of Employment and Productivity. (The DEP was the old Ministry of Labour with the added responsibility for prices and incomes policy and for improving productivity except in its purely technological aspects.)

At the Prime Minister's request, she proceeded to formulate the government's intentions which were embodied in a White Paper (Cmnd 3888), published in January 1969, and entitled In Place of Strife. As if in mockery of its title, it caused more strife within the Labour Party than any other document emanating from a Labour government since the war. The intention of the government was not to humiliate or shackle the unions, but to oust as far as possible unofficial strikes. The unions did not quarrel with this aim, but were furious that the legislation which was proposed, contained penal clauses which in certain circumstances would make employers, unions or individuals liable to fines.

When the subject was debated in early March, 53 Labour MPs voted against the proposals and later in the month, the party's National Executive Committee rejected them. The Cabinet too was split in the matter, Jim Callaghan leading the opposition to the proposals.

Not even Harold Wilson, with Barbara Castle's powerful backing, could steam-roller this one through the House of Commons, as he had incomes policy, without creating the biggest split in the party since 1931. On 18 June, an agreement was reached with the unions which was held by Harold Wilson and Barbara Castle to obviate the need for legislation. Put another way, Harold Wilson and Barbara Castle decided that they had no alternative but to surrender to the unions. They agreed to withdraw their proposals after a "solemn and binding" undertaking by the unions to use their influence to curb unofficial strikes. How "solemn" was the undertaking is hardly something which can be measured. It certainly never proved binding and "Mr Solomon Binding" became a figure for caustic jests for some time to come. Was it, one may wonder, any consolation to Harold Wilson to know that, though he had failed to win fame as a tamer of the unions, he had at least demonstrated to the world his prowess as a political escapologist?

The passage of time made an early peace between government and unions imperative for Labour. It was now more than three years since the 1966 election and it was not too early to keep their eyes open for a favourable moment to go to the country again.

By expunging In Place of Strife from the political agenda and terminating incomes policy, the Labour leaders had restored at least a surface peace even though all the major industrial relations problems remained unresolved. They could go to the country with a semblance of unity. Moreover, good news was now coming from the economic front, as the improvement in the balance of payments achieved in 1969 continued into 1970.

In April, Jenkins introduced what many people thought would be a pre-election budget in content as well as in timing. They were wrong about the contents, but not about the timing. There was no hint in it of trying to buy votes. Concessions were made in personal tax allowances, but these did little more than offset the amount which would have accrued to the Inland Revenue as rising inflation dragged more and more wage earners into the lower tax range. The net effect of the budget was neutral.

Even in the absence of budgetary inducements, there was much to be said from Labour's stand-point for a 1970 election before the wages/prices spiral got out of hand, whilst the pound was still strong and whilst the balance of payments was still in the black. Local election results virtually clinched the matter. Labour had their best results since 1964, confirming recent opinion polls which had shown that, despite having at one time trailed behind the Conservatives by 22.5%, they were now slightly ahead. It was, therefore, no surprise when shortly after the local election results were known, Wilson announced that there would be a general election on 18 June.

Their election manifesto, "Now Britain's Strong - Let's make her Great to Live in", understandably emphasised their achievement in transforming her balance of payments from a (supposed) deficit of £800 million to a surplus of £1,3000 million. They also claimed credit for re-organising and re-equipping the employment services (see p 153) so that they could move in more quickly to deal with redundancies and for carrying out "the biggest expansion in industrial training in Britain's history".

The Conservatives felt themselves equally well-prepared for office. At a series of 'get-togethers", culminating in the Selsdon Park (Croydon) Conference early in January 1970, they had hammered out the policies they meant to pursue once in office. Ever since the war, they affirmed, there had been too much "nannying" of the people by both Labour and Conservative governments. These latter-day Conservatives would break with the formularies of the past and, in the words of their manifesto, "A Better Tomorrow": "cut public expenditure, liberate industry from state interference and allow market forces to determine which industries should prosper and which decline."

Had the election been taking place ten years earlier, the existence of 600,000 unemployed would have brought obloquy on the heads of the incumbent government and cries of horror from the parties trying to oust them. But, as the politicians were no doubt aware, the general public had come to accept this sort of figure as normal.

Nevertheless, unemployment at 2.4% was now a more important issue than when it had stood at only 1.2% at the previous election. David Butler found that 76% of Conservative candidates mentioned it in their election addresses, compared with only 12% of Labour candidates. Labour was clearly much more on the defensive in this matter than they had been in 1966 when the figures were 8% and 16% respectively.

The Conservatives pressed the matter home in their manifesto: "The nation now knows," it declared, "what five years of Labour rule can mean. Hundreds of thousands of extra families suffering the hardship and insecurity of unemployment." However, they felt no need to propose specific measures to promote a high general level of employment. That would follow as a corollary to running the economy more efficiently.

Neither Labour nor Conservatives could ignore the problem of the less fortunate regions, though neither party put forward any radical proposals for dealing with them. The Conservatives, though letting it be known that they would phase out Regional Employment Premiums, proclaimed that they would make greater use of the powers given by Local Employment Acts and pay special attention to the needs of the development areas in their plans for a "massive increase in retraining facilities". Labour criticised the Conservatives for their intention to phase out Regional Employment Premiums and promised a continuance of past policies. "A Labour Government," they declared, "has pursued and will pursue a vigorous policy of regional development."

What people were really worried about was inflation, retail prices having risen by 5½% in the year before the election. Despite the vulnerability of Labour on this important matter for most of the campaign, they seemed to be gliding to certain victory. Nor was their confidence shaken by what must have seemed a rather unkind blow of fortune just three days before polling: trade figures were published showing a deficit during May of £31 million, an out-turn quite out of keeping with the returns for many months past and to come. The Conservatives made the most of these figures, which may well have aroused doubts in the minds of some uncommitted voters as to whether Labour's claim to have got the balance of payments under control was really as well-grounded as they asserted.

But there were few doubts in the minds of the Labour faithful when polling day arrived. Only one of the major pollsters (Opinion Research Centre) predicted a Conservative victory and that by as little as 1%. History does not record how many shivers ran down how many Labour backs when the first results, announced from Guildford, showed a 6% swing to Conservatives. Unless this was a freak result - and why should it be? - a Conservative victory was assured. So it proved to be. The United Kingdom swing to the Conservatives (4.7%) was rather less than at Guildford, but enough to give them a comfortable lead over all other parties, as Table 10 below shows.

Table 10

Gereral Election of 18th June 1970

Party	Votes Received	Percentage Votes	Number of MPs
Conservatives	13,145,123	46.4	330
Labour	12,179,341	43.0	287
Liberals	2,117,035	7.5	6
Others	903,299	3.1	7

A Sort of Calm, June - Dec 1970
The Conservatives had every right to be delighted with the election result. Victory is all the sweeter when it confounds the prophets. In particular, it was a personal triumph for Edward Heath, who, like the general who wins the last battle, had been victorious when it mattered most. He had not only discomfited his opponents but also (for the time being!) silenced the critics within his own party.

Fate seemed to be smiling. On the wider front, the General having departed the political scene in France, the prospects were good that Britain would soon be admitted to the European Economic Community. No one would have more reason to rejoice when that came about than Heath himself who, as Britain's chief negotiator when Macmillan was Prime Minister, had slogged away for so many weary months with little apparent reward.

In domestic affairs he had inherited from Labour a healthy balance of payments surplus whilst, with unemployment at 2.4%, there was enough slack in the labour market to provide some flexibility, but not so much, having regard to the new ambivalence about how much unemployment was acceptable, as to cause alarm.

If Fate was smiling, the smile was sardonic. What was in store was not a smooth transition from a state dominated to a free enterprise economy, but a bone-rattling ride to economic failure and electoral defeat.

The first of Fate's hammer blows fell when the government had been in office scarcely a month. Iain Macleod, the new Chancellor of the Exchequer and arguably the most able of the Conservative front-benchers, died of a heart attack on 20 July. His place was taken by the comparatively unknown Anthony Barber. It is difficult to believe that had Macleod lived a few years longer, the course of government would have run quite as disastrously as it did.

The Conservatives entered office committed to giving the country a "New Style of Government". There would be "less government and better government carried out by fewer people". This, it was hoped, would result in "liberating private initiatives and placing more responsibility on the individual and less on the state".

There were three early priorities which they set before themselves: the reorganisation of central government; the dismantling of many of Labour's interventionist bodies and a reduction in the level of pay awards. They also began to tackle the problem of local authority functions and boundaries, although the form their reforms would take was not fully evident until legislation was passed in 1972 for England and Wales and 1973 for Scotland. Despite having before them recommendations of Royal Commissions for England and Wales under lord Redcliffe-Maud and under Lord Wheatley for Scotland, their final proposals were essentially of their own devising.

The nature of their reorganisation of central government was set out in a White Paper (Cmnd 4506) published in October 1970. A major feature of this reorganisation was the amalgamation of several Ministeries under two large ones, the Department of Trade and Industry and the Department of the Environment. The Department of Employment and Productivity became simply the Department of Employment. State intervention in productivity matters was to cease; such things in the future would have to be settled between employers and employees.

A new entity in the apparatus of government was the Central Policy Review Staff established in 1970 with Lord Rothschild as its first Chairman. Heath called it his "central capability" unit, its role being to review in long term perspective matters referred to it by the Cabinet and to examine subjects which cut across departmental boundaries. It lasted until Mrs Thatcher abolished it in 1983, but never quite achieved the hopes placed in it largely because most government, Heath's included, spend most of their time and effort on matters which affect their standing in current opinion polls or which have relevance to the next election.

The first assault on Labour's interventionist devices was announced by Anthony Barber in October 1970 when he introduced his first budget. The Industrial Reorganisation Corporation was to be wound up, Selective Employment Tax to be phased out, and the Regional Employment Premium to be terminated in 1974, i.e. as soon as the seven year period promised by Labour had been reached, and investment grants were to be replaced by investment allowances. A few weeks later, it was announced that the National Board for Prices and Incomes would be wound up.

The government were now without any formal incomes policy or official machinery for determining pay levels. This was fully consistent with the non-interventionist policy proclaimed in their election manifesto and reiterated in November 1970 by John Davis, Secretary of State for Trade and Industry, who told the House of Commons that the country needed to "gear its policies to the great majority of the people who are not lame ducks, who do not need a hand, who are quite capable of looking after their own interests and only ask to be allowed to do so".

Though without any formal incomes policy, the government had a definite aim, embodied in its 'N minus 1' target, i.e. the idea of reducing by 1% each successive wage settlement in which the government had a say. Although this aim was never achieved, settlements during the first year following the election with the electricity suppliers, local authorities and postal workers were not greatly out of line with government hopes.

Little was heard at this time about unemployment. Neither Labour nor Conservatives considered it to be high enough to merit formal debate nor did the matter figure at all prominently in Barber's presentation of his first budget on 27 October. In it he announced cuts in public expenditure amounting to £329 million, roughly matched by a reduction in the standard rate of income tax from 8s 3d to 7s 9d, and in Corporation Tax from 45% to 42%. From an employment point of view it seemed an appropriate budget for the time.

Unemployment Takes Off, Jan 1971 - Aug 1972

First overt sign that the long stability in unemployment levels might be breaking down occurred in December when against the seasonal trend, the head count of unemployed rose by 20,000. The government were now on the horns of a very sharp dilemma. They had assumed office in 1970 as firmly committed to checking the rise in prices as the Wilson government had been in 1964 to increasing the rate of economic growth. The way that employment was now going demanded reflation, the speed at which prices were rising deflation.

It was easy enough to see the long-term solution which was to raise the economy to such a new pitch of efficiency that the rise in productivity matched the rise in prices. Meanwhile, the government had to deal with the current situation in which the sharp rise in unemployment was arousing strong emotions both in Parliament and country.

Understandably, therefore, Barber's second budget, presented on 30 March 1971, constituted a notable departure from the neutral budget he had introduced five months earlier. Incentives to individuals were granted by reliefs in direct taxation and to companies by a reduction in SET and Corporation Tax. He also outlined measures which he intended to introduce later, including the replacement of purchase tax by VAT and the recasting of income tax.

The Chancellor did not disguise the fact that his major concern was the "high and rising unemployment combined with cost inflation". "If," he told the House, "the measures I am about to announce have been allowed a reasonable time to take effect and a further stimulus is needed, the usual instruments are available."

Rising unemployment and the redundancies and fears of redundancies which went with it, were now putting the government to a severe test. In February 1971, Rolls Royce declared themselves to be insolvent. What had happened was this. In 1968 (amid great rejoicings on the British side) Rolls Royce had won a contract against fierce competition from the American companies, General Electric and Pratt and Whitney, to supply engines (the RB211s) for the new Lockhead Trident aircraft. Unfortunately, they had undertaken to supply them at a fixed price, but with the general rise in prices and soaring development costs, were finding this undertaking impossible to fulfil.

The company had been in financial difficulties for some years and, despite assistance from Labour in their late and Conservatives in their early months of office, had cut their labour force by 5,000 during 1970. Strict adherence to the "lame duck" policy would have meant putting in jeopardy the jobs of 80,000 Rolls Royce employees and thousands more in sub-contracting firms and main suppliers.

Little wonder that rather than face all this, the government decided to nationalise the company. Redundancies ensued, but on a far smaller scale than would have occurred without government intervention. Early in March, Rolls Royce announced that 4,300 workers would be made redundant, principally from Derby, where the company's headquarters were located, and from Scotland. Amongst suppliers, Lucas were the most severely hit. On 9 February, 8,000 of their employees were put on a three-day week and three days later, they announced that redundancies would amount to nearly 3,000.

Rescue of Rolls Royce by a government supposedly dedicated to laissez-faire policies could plausibly be justified on defence grounds. No government, it might be argued, could allow a company working on military contracts vital to national security, to go to the wall because of difficulties in its civilian work.

Defence considerations were less to the fore in the case of Upper Clyde Shipbuilders. Only one of the five companies forming this group, Yarrow Shipbuilders, had substantial defence contracts. The government made a grant of £4 million to enable them to complete these contracts. The appeal of the other four companies was refused. Instead, the government appointed a Committee under Lord Robens to make recommendations on the future of these yards.

Lord Roben's report, received on 29 July, recommended that two of the yards should be closed and the other two retained and modernised. This would have meant the immediate redundancy of 400 men and ultimately, anything up to 6,000. When a few days later, the government indicated its intention to implement this Report, workers immediately occupied all four yards and refused to be moved. Through television and the press, the faces and voices of James Reid and James Airlie, the shop stewards who had organised this action, became familiar throughout the United Kingdom. To most people, a worker's sit in was a novel phenomenon, some regarding it as a dangerous exercise in lawlessness, others as a brave defence of workers' rights.

The government delayed making any final decision about the future of UCS whilst desperate efforts to find new orders and new clients were made. Eventually, the Marathon Manufacturing Company of Texas, encouraged by the prospect of grants under a new Industry Act, agreed to place an order for oil rigs at Clydebank, whilst the remaining three yards were formed into a new entity, Govan Shipbuilders. It was announced on 28 February 1972, that the government would inject £3.5 million into this new company.

By the time the UCS affair was settled (to pop up again under later governments) unemployment and the emotions it engendered were at their peak and on 21 March, Barber presented the most expansionist of all his budgets. £1,200 million were remitted in taxation whilst the budget deficit was allowed to increase to an expected £2,441 million.

More memorable than the facts and figures in this budget was Barber's statement on future policy: "I am sure," he told his audience, "that all honourable members in this House agree that the lesson of international balance of payments upsets in the last few years is that it is neither necessary nor desirable to distort domestic economies to an unacceptable extent in order to maintain unrealistic exchange rates whether they are too high or too low."

Circumstances in the summer provided a specially suitable opportunity to "free the pound". The international agreement on fixed exchange rates reached at Bretton Woods in 1944, was already crumbling largely as a result of the weakening of the dollar due to the Vietnam War and the comparatively poor performance of the American economy. On 23 June 1972, following a considerable outflow of short-term capital from Britain, Barber announced that the pound would be allowed to float.

In September Bank Rate, which had been lowered from 7 1/2% to 6% in April, was reduced to 5%, ceiling limits on bank lending were removed and important changes were made in the regulations covering lending by banks and other institutions. The object of these relaxations was to facilitate changes emanating from 'Competition and Credit Control', a consultative document published by the Bank of England the previous May. From 16 September, instead of being subject to quantitive ceilings on lending, the banks and larger finance houses simply undertook to observe minimum reserves of "eligible liabilities", amounting to 12 1/2% for the former and 10% for the latter. They also agreed to place such deposits with the Bank of England as might be called for from time to time.

Unfortunately much of the credit engendered by these innovations overflowed into property speculation and secondary banking; it made little contribution towards modernising British industry. Nor did it create jobs, least of all for the manual workers who were bearing the main brunt of the high unemployment. Whilst the tempo of activity in the money markets quickened, it stagnated in the labour market. In contrast to their silence about unemployment a year earlier, both Labour and Conservative parties debated the matter at their 1971 Conferences, the Labour Party passing a resolution that the return to full employment should be a "first priority" of the next Labour government.

Not surprisingly, the TUC too at their Conference in September, took the government to task for allowing unemployment to rise so sharply, their favoured nostrum for this malady being "a shorter working week, longer holidays, more public holidays and early retirement".

When Parliament reassembled after the summer recess, another 7,500 had been added to the unemployment total. The opposition naturally lost no time in going into the attack. During the debate on the Royal Address, Roy Jenkins moved to add the words, "but humbly regret that the Gracious Speech makes no recognition of the worst unemployment for a generation and puts forward no coherent strategy to deal with this and other economic problems". Six days later, Barbara Castle moved a motion that "this House deplores the continuing failure of the policies of the government which have led to the present intolerable level of unemployment".

Barber's riposte that the measures taken by the government to reflate the economy during the last nine months were "certainly far greater than anything undertaken by any previous government" was as true as it was ineffectual in turning away wrath. Nevertheless, in order to show beyond any doubt the government's determination to bring unemployment down, he went on to announce an acceleration in government expenditure by £185 million over the next two years.

The anger about unemployment was not confined to expressions within Parliament. The TUC called on their members to lobby their MPs on the day of the unemployment debate (23 November 1971). On that day, a massive march of protesters took place, straining to the utmost police efforts to keep the crowds under control, impeding MPs as they went about their business and holding up proceedings in the Commons for a full hour.

Early in December, Barber announced that all outstanding post-war credits would be repaid. This did not stop the unemployment total from rising to 967,000 in December. If the normal post-Christmas rise took place, the head count of unemployed in January would exceed a million for the first time since the 1946 Insurance Act came into effect. This is exactly what happened, the January total being 1,024,000. The February total, 1,621,000, looked infinitely worse. In fact, it was very little different from the January figure as 653,000 of this total were only temporarily stopped. (At that time, temporarily stopped workers were still included in the official count of unemployed if they happened to be laid off on the day of the count. This practice was stopped later in the year and the temporarily stopped, though noted as a separate figure, were no longer included in the total.)

It is interesting to note how this million total was reached. Hitherto, the national unemployment total issued by the Ministry of Labour/Department of Employment was that for Great Britain. Recently the Department had issued figures both for G.B. and U.K. The media, at a time when unemployment was dramatic news, naturally latched on to the larger (over one million) U.K. figures rather than the smaller (just under one million) G.B. figure.

By the time Barber introduced his next budget on 21 March 1972, the latest count (for U.K. and including the temporarily stopped) still showed over a million. Responding to the bombardment of criticism being fired at him in the House, Barber made it clear that the reduction of unemployment was still his top priority. "I have never looked to unemployment," he told Members, "as the cure for inflation." He attributed the high total at that time to slow economic growth in 1970, the fall in output in 1971 and the "so-called shake out" of labour which had occurred in industry.

His aim was to raise the growth rate in the coming year from the projected 3% to 5%. In view of the government's oft-repeated aim to keep expenditure down, the Chancellor decided to achieve this object by reductions in personal tax allowances and the lowering of purchase tax. Net revenue, it was estimated, would be down by £1.2 billion in the year 1972-73, making the 1972 budget one of the most expansionary ever introduced by a British Chancellor. It gave a major fillip to what became known as the "Barber boom".

Because the boom got out of hand in 1973, and augmented the inflationary pressures of that year, the 1972 budget has been much criticised in retrospect. The Chancellor should have seen, it was said, that measures already taken, plus the natural upturn of the business cycle, would have ensured a rise in production and fall in unemployment without any additional stimulus by the government. At the time, there were few critics to tell him so.

By this time the unemployment figures were beginning to stabilise and from August onwards, the government had a new and powerful instrument to fight any relapse. This was the Industry Act 1972, which though primarily designed to stimulate production and unemployment in assisted areas, also gave the government, under Section 8, powers to provide financial assistance to industry whenever it is "in the national interest" and "wherever it is likely to benefit the economy of the United Kingdom".

The battle over unemployment was almost at an end, but the battle over incomes policy and the Industrial Relations Act was still raging.

Boom and Bust, Sept 1972 - Feb 1974.

The furore about unemployment died down almost as quickly as it had flared up. This was partly because from the autumn of 1972 it was falling steadily and partly because public and media attention was increasingly focused on those two other bones of contention - the Industrial Relations Bill and incomes policy. Neither of these bitter conflicts impinged directly on the employment situation although both separately and collectively they damaged the economic health of the country and therewith its future wealth and job creating capability.

One of the regrettable effects of the well-intentioned but disastrous Industrial Relations Bill was to rule out any consensus approach to problem solving. This was clearly evident in the month before the Bill was passed. In July 1971, the CBI, at government prompting, obtained the agreement of nearly all its larger members to limit price increases to 5% for the twelve months following. The hope was that the unions would follow suit and inflationary pressures be significantly weakened. The unions, working themselves up into a fury over the Industrial Relations Bill, now nearing the end of its storm-tossed passage through the Houses of Parliament, refused to modify either pay claims or polemics.

The Conservatives had set out their intentions very clearly in their election manifesto in which they had stated: "We will introduce a comprehensive Industrial Relations Bill in the first session of the new Parliament. It will provide a proper framework of law within which improved relationships between management and unions can take place."

Ironically in the light of events, it continued, "we aim to create conditions in which strikes become the means of last resort, not of first resort, as so often now". What actually happened was that (as shown in Table 9, p 57) working days lost by strikes rose from 11.0 million in 1970 to 13.6 million in 1971 and 23.9 million in 1972, the first full calendar year after the Bill was passed. It is true that they dropped to 7.2 million in 1973, but even that was higher than any of the five complete years of the recent Labour government.

The Bill had been introduced to the House of Commons in December 1970 and received the Royal Assent in August 1971, having survived the longest Committee stage of any non-finance Bill since the war, a national "day of protest" organised by the TUC and sundry other demonstrations and outbursts up and down the country.

Although the Act placed a number of constraints on unions (and employers) it also offered some advantages. But to obtain these a union would have to register with a new body, the Register of Employers, Trade Unions and Employers Associations.

The government assumed that the advantages of registering were sufficient to induce most unions to do so. They were wrong. The TUC let its members know that they risked expulsion if they did so and passed a resolution to that effect at their annual Conference in September 1972. Only a handful of unions did in fact register, thereby undermining the efficacy of the Act right from the start. When the government wanted to bring the unions into consultation on the formulation of an incomes policy, it constituted an impassable barrier to any sort of reasonable dialogue.

Unlike the Industrial Relations Act, the statutory incomes policy introduced by the government constituted a complete U-turn from the undertaking in the party's election manifesto, "Labour's compulsory wage control was a failure and we will not repeat it."

The decision to perform this embarrassing manoeuvre was not made suddenly and was reached reluctantly after more than six months of abortive negotiations with the TUC. It was precipitated by the acceleration in the rise in prices (5.4% in 1969, 6.4% in 1970 and 9.4% in 1971) and the demolition by the miners of the government's N-1 policy.

The miners had for several years been sliding down the earnings league table and in the generally more militant climate of the early seventies, were determined to reverse this trend. A strike started on 9

January 1972 and ended on 18 February, only after an enquiry under Lord Wilberforce had, on the government's admission, awarded rises in minimum weekly pay-rates of 27.8% for surface and 31.6% for underground miners.

The government's pay policy was now in ruins and it was shortly after this that they opened negotiations with the unions on a voluntary basis. Various concessions were offered, but not the only one which would have clinched the matter - repeal of the Industrial Relations Act. This was a price which even a government in retreat were not prepared to pay and on 6 November, pride having been swallowed, Heath announced in the House of Commons that the government intended to introduce a statutory incomes policy, Phase 1 of which would take the form of a 90 day freeze on both pay and prices.

Under Phase 2 of incomes policy, which began in March 1973, pay increases were limited to £1 plus 4% with an overall maximum annual increase of £250. Practiced now in U-turns, the government established a Pay Board and Prices Commission. Success of any pay policy depends not only on its contents but also on the industrial relations climate and other circumstances of the time when it is in operation. The industrial relations climate in 1973 could hardly have been worse, whilst the turmoil which arose on that score was aggravated by a number of other economic factors.

First was the government's own mis-reading of the situation. When Barber introduced his 1973 budget early in March, production was already expanding at a rate which should have caused unease if not alarm. What was required was a budget which would restrain without halting expansion. But the memory of recent high unemployment was still fresh and what the country got was a budget which was broadly neutral, its main features being the already promised introduction of VAT at 10% and the abolition of purchase tax and selective employment tax.

Second, was the boom in world trade, the stimulus of which to British exports was more than offset by the rise in commodity prices. Between the third quarter of 1972 and the third quarter of 1973, export prices rose by 13%, import prices by 32%.

Finally, there was the turmoil in international money markets which accompanied a sharp rise in the American balance of payments deficit.

The government were now bedevilled by a situation exactly the reverse of that in late 1971 and early 1972. Because of the time-lag between the enactment of expansionary measures and their impact on the economy, they were unable in the earlier period to get output rising quickly enough to absorb the unemployed. By the middle of 1973, the economy was expanding at a speed which could not be moderated quickly enough to curb inflation.

Steps taken to halt this gallop to disaster were ineffectual and late. In May, the Chancellor announced that he would cut estimated expenditure in 1973-74 by £100 million and in 1974-75 by £500 million. In July, Minimum Lending Rate (which since reorganisation in the City had taken the place of Bank Rate) was raised from 7 1/2% to 11 1/2% - up to that time a record. This lasted only until November when it was raised once again to 13%.

For the second time in the Heath ministry events pivoted round what the miners were going to do. At their annual Conference in July, the National Union of Mineworkers demanded wage increases ranging from 22% to 47%. The government could not, without openly renouncing their own pay policy, allow the National Coal Board to settle for that or anything like that amount. Yet they were desperately anxious to devise some means which would allow the miners to settle with dignity but which would not open the floodgates to a shoal of other needy or greedy claimants.

For that reason Stage III of incomes policy, which came into effect early in November 1973, was a more complex affair than its predecessors. Included in it was a clause about unsocial hours, i.e.

that "those who worked whilst the rest of the world was sleeping or at play", could claim an extra pay rise, a formula which seemed specially tailored to meet the special circumstances of the miners. Settlements not qualifying for the unsocial hours provisions or one or two other allowances of a minor nature were limited to a 7% increase with an overall annual maximum of £350.

Because of events unforeseen and perhaps unforeseeable at the time, all these provisions were subordinate in importance to the escalator clauses under which every 1% increase in the retail price index beyond 7% would entitle each employee to an additional 40p in weekly pay. By an ironic twist of fate, Stage III was announced on 8 October only two days after the outbreak of the Arab-Israeli war, an event destined to promote world-wide inflation, engender the worst international recession since the second world war and vastly increase the burden of Third World indebtedness.

Between the middle of October and the end of December, the posted price of oil rose from $3 to $11.65 a barrel.

One effect of this quite unprecedented rise in oil prices was to augment the bargaining power of the miners. If the price of oil was to soar, so too, they argued, must the value of what they produced, just as its value had declined when cheap oil, cheap gas and the spread of nuclear power stations, ousted coal from its ancient primacy in the provision of energy.

Events moved quickly to a climax. By mid-November, the miners and electricity supply workers had started separate overtime bans and the government had declared a State of Emergency. For good measure, on 12 December, ASLEF, the engine drivers' union, started a work-to-rule and on the following day, the government declared that, to conserve fuel supplies, industry would be put on a three-day week in the New Year.

The TUC, who were as keen to conserve members' earnings as to

77

'bash' the government, made it known in the second week of January that if the miners were allowed to breach the Stage III limits, other unions would be prepared to regard the miners as a special case and would refrain from using any settlement made with them as an argument in favour of their own claims. Whether through blindness, obstinacy or the belief (which certainly had some substance) that the TUC could not deliver, the government brushed this offer aside.

Another possible chance of a settlement with the miners was missed when, on 24 January, the Pay Board recommended that a Relativities Board be established to examine, amongst other things, whether any group of workers were being underpaid and should, therefore, be considered as a special case. In view of the TUC's anxiety for a settlement and the near-certainty that a Relativities Board would add something to what the government (through the Coal Board) were offering the miners, appointment of such a Board might well have opened a way to agreement.

The government remained unmoved and the two parties were still deadlocked when, on 5 February, having received support from 81% of their membership in a national ballot, the NUM announced that they would bring their members out on strike in five days time. This seemed to Heath to have brought to an end any chance of a negotiated settlement. After initial hesitation and after sounding out his senior Ministers, he declared that a general election would be held on 28 February.

Despite the urgings of some of his colleagues, it had never been Heath's wish to conduct an election on the theme "Who controls the country, the elected government or the unions?" Inevitably, however, this was the question which cropped up time and again during the campaign. This theme was, of course, very meaningful to the electors as inflation was their biggest worry and it was widely held that the main cause for constantly rising prices was union-inspired wage demands.

Labour hoped to convince electors that they could deal with this matter more effectively than the Conservatives because of the accord they had reached with the unions whilst in opposition. Under this agreement, known as the "social contract", the Labour party undertook once in office to repeal the Industrial Relations Act and implement other requests from the unions; the unions in turn would endeavour to keep wage settlements down to what was necessary to compensate for price increases and to ensure that there was a twelve month interval between major settlements.

Unemployment was a very subordinate issue. Forgotten were the trauma and excitements of 1971 and 1972. Since then the belated impact of the government's expansionary measures, buoyant world trade (until the oil crisis of 1973) and the new flexibility of the pound, had combined to produce a high level of demand for labour. Vacancies notified to employment exchanges and Careers Offices were at their highest level for seven years, whilst unemployment in December had fallen to 1.9%, the last recorded occasion on which it has been below 2%. It is true that both the January and February figures (released a few days before polling) showed slight rises, but this, it seemed at the time, could reasonably be attributed to the dislocations arising from the three-day week, which would be terminated once normality in industry was restored.

Parliamentary candidates seemed to share this unconcern about unemployment. In his survey of election addresses, Butler found that only 16% of Conservative and 17% of Labour candidates even mentioned the subject.

Nor did it receive much prominence in the election manifestos of either of the main parties. The Conservatives in "Firm Action for a Fair Britain", limited themselves to stressing the boost they would give to training and the benefits that would flow to the Regions from the Industry Act of 1972.

Labour, in their manifesto, "Let us work together - Labour's way out of the crisis", were not quite as laconic. "The Tories," they said, "have brought the country to the edge of bankruptcy and breakdown. More and more people are losing their jobs. Firms are going out of business. Labour would promote employment in the hard-pressed parts of the country by the new REGIONAL PLANNING MACHINERY and would increase social equality by giving far greater importance to full employment and social benefits."

The result of the election was almost a tie between the two main parties, as the figures in Table 11 below show.

Table 11

General Election of 28th February 1974

Party	Votes Received	Percentage Votes	Number of MPs
Labour	11,639,243	37.1	301
Conservatives	11,868,906	37.9	297
Liberals	6,063,470	19.3	14
Others	1,762,047	5.7	23

Statistically there is one striking parallel between this election result and that of 1951. In both elections, about 230,000 voters separated the two main parties and in both elections, the party with the lower popular vote (Conservatives in 1951, Labour in 1974) won the greater number of seats. More significant, perhaps, was the decline since 1970 in popular backing for both main parties. Conservative support fell from 46.4% of all votes cast to 37.9% and Labour support from 43.0% to 37.1%.

In the years between, voters had become more volatile and perhaps more cynical about the two main contenders. One effect of this more

80

censorious attitude was a surge in backing for the Scottish and Welsh nationalist parties which together polled over 700,000 votes. Because of the "first past the post" anomalies of the British electoral system, this won for them only seven and two seats respectively. The scales of justice were tilted even more grotesquely against the Liberals, support for whom had risen from 7.5% of the votes cast in 1970 to 19.3% in 1974. They had to be content with only 14 out of 635 seats in the House of Commons.

Following the announcement of the poll results, Heath made an abortive attempt to form a coalition with the Liberals, but when this failed, had to concede defeat.

Regional and Urban Unemployment, 1964-74.
Regional Unemployment.

As mentioned earlier, Labour looked to the reserves in the high unemployment regions to enable them to reach the targets set in the National Plan. The Plan, much discussed in the early months of the new administration, but not published till September 1965, estimated that productivity should grow at 3.2% a year between 1964 and 1970. As this alone would be insufficient to achieve the 25% growth rate aimed at over this period, it would be necessary to expand the labour force by 800,000.

Much of this labour would perforce have to come from those parts of the country where there was a surplus of manpower. If, the Plan pointed out, unemployment in the regions of labour surplus was reduced to the GB average for the last ten years, about 100,000 more persons would be employed in them, 37,000 in Scotland, 28,000 in Northern Ireland and 12,000 each in the North West, the North and Wales.

The Regional Planning which was to bring about this happy turn of events was the responsibility of a special Division of the Department of Economic Affairs. Under its direction, the country was divided into Eight Planning Regions for England and one each for Scotland and Wales. Each region had a Planning Council and a Planning Board. The Planning Councils consisted of approximately 26 members ("part-time, non-elected worthies" as they have been described), a third drawn from industry (both employer and union sides), a third from local authorities and a third from other organisations such as the Universities. They were served by a small number of senior civil servants, mostly on a part-time basis, seconded from their departments.

Although supposed to represent general regional interests, their most important task to begin with was to produce Regional Plans which would dovetail into the National Plan. Despite the early demise of the National Plan, and later of the DEA itself, Regional Planning was not abandoned, but its primacy in the scheme of things was greatly diminished.

If the government were to make a real impact on the regional problem, they would have to pass new legislation. Meanwhile, they could apply existing legislation more rigorously than the Conservatives had done. This they did, making industrial development certificates mandatory for all manufacturing projects of 1,000 square feet or more and by showing themselves far less ready than the Conservatives had been to allow new projects into the crowded South and Midlands. By the end of their first year in office, expenditure on industrial estates and advance factories had more than doubled and sixteen new areas had been added to the list of Development Districts.

In August 1966, the government passed their Industrial Development Act. Development Districts were abolished and five Development Areas created in their place. These five Development Areas covered in whole or in part Scotland, Wales, the North of England, Merseyside and Cornwall together with West Devon. Whereas the Development Districts had been chosen entirely on their unemployment levels, the new Areas were chosen on the grounds of population change, migration and employment structure, as well as the level of unemployment.

A major aim of government was to increase capital investment throughout the country and to this end a 20% grant was made available towards investment in manufacturing industry throughout the country. In the Development Areas this grant was set at 40% (later changed to 45% in Development Areas and 25% elsewhere). The 25% grant towards building costs which had been available in Development Districts remained unchanged in the Development Areas, but was not available outside these Areas. Further inducements to firms to open up or expand in Development Areas, included the provision of factory space for sale or rent at reasonable prices and financial assistance from the Ministry of Labour towards the cost of training.

During 1967, three additional steps to promote Regional Development were announced: the introduction of a Regional Employment Premium (REP); the designation of certain Special Development Areas; and the appointment of what became known as the Hunt Committee (so called because Sir Joseph Hunt was the Chairman).

The Regional Employment Premium enabled employers in manufacturing industry in the Development Areas (DAs) to claim a rebate of thirty shillings a week for each adult male employee (rather less for women and young persons). Until the 7/6 SET rebate available to manufacturing employers in all parts of the country was abolished, following devaluation, employers in the DAs could claim rebates on both SET and REP. When SET was abolished, employers in DAs continued to receive REP. The government's hope was that by lowering labour costs of firms in the DAs, they would make them more competitive. It was also hoped that the introduction of REP would go some way towards meeting the criticism often made that existing regional aids were concentrated too much on capital intensive industry when what was needed was labour intensive projects which would mop up some of the surplus labour in these areas. To give employers some assurance that the scheme would not, as some former schemes, be abruptly terminated, the government let it be known that it would not be withdrawn before 1974.

The new category of Special Development Areas was created to deal with the aftermath of pit closures now gathering momentum. (The coalmining labour force shrank by nearly 30% between 1963 and 1968). Very often these closures left villages or small towns virtually without employment, except for a few basic services. Scotland, Wales, North East England and West Cumberland were the parts most affected. In these areas, factories on industrial sites could be used rent-free for five years (two years in Development Areas), building grants of 35% (25% in DAs) were available and operational grants (not available in DAs) could be negotiated to cover the first few difficult years of production.

The task given to the Hunt Committee was that of examining the problem of the grey or intermediate areas which, though not qualifying for Development Area status, were substantially below the national average in employment prospects, income per head, outward migration rate and other criteria by which local well-being is judged. The introduction of REP in Development Areas only increased the long existing sense of grievance in the grey areas at being as much shut out from DA benefits as were the prosperous South and Midlands.

This sense of grievance was understandable, as was the government's caution in doing anything about it. Already 20% of the country's population lived in parts of the country with Development Area status. Nevertheless, the Hunt Committee, reporting in April 1969, recommended that these intermediate areas should receive most of the grants available in Development Areas. Almost a year later, under the Local Employment Act 1970, seven such areas, ranging from Scotland to the South West of England, were designated Intermediate Areas and qualified for grants similar to those available in DAs.

These measures were not effective enough to stop the Conservatives in their 1970 election manifesto taking Labour to task for failing to prevent the sharp rise in unemployment which occurred in the less fortunate regions, and in Scotland and Wales. "We are not prepared," they declared, "to tolerate the human waste and suffering that accompany persistent unemployment, dereliction and decline." Though not deflected from their long announced intention to do away with the Regional Employment Premium, they promised to make greater use of the powers given by the Local Employment Acts and "to give special attention to the needs of the Development Areas in our plans for a massive increase in retraining facilities".

More details of their intentions were given in a White Paper (Cmnd 4516) published in October 1970. This Paper reflected the long-held Conservative view that investment allowances (which rewarded only those firms which made a profit) were a better inducement to employers than Labour's investment grants (which benefit the competent and incompetent alike). They therefore intended to substitute 100% depreciation allowances for plant and machinery in the Development Areas and 60% allowances in the rest of the country for Labour's investment grants. The government also announced that it would increase the discretionary aid to which assisted areas were already entitled under the Local Employment Acts. More too would be spent on infrastructure.

The hope was that these limited increases in government aid would be more than paid for by the spurt in investment which would ensue from an expanding economy. The higher the level of investment elsewhere, the greater would be the competition for labour and other resources and the more reason for entrepreneurs to look to parts of the country where these things were available.

Unfortunately, within only a few months, this policy was brought to nought as production stagnated and unemployment rose over the whole country. In February 1971, the government, recognising that these early hopes would not now be realised, announced that Glasgow, Tyneside and Wear and parts of South Wales would be designated Special Development Areas. About 8.5% of the insured population now lived in SDAs, compared with 1.8% before. In March, Intermediate Area status was conceded to Edinburgh and small portions of the West Midlands and Yorks and Humberside.

Because of the growing concern at the nationwide rise in unemployment in July 1971, the government raised the initial allowances for plant and machinery from 60% to 80% in all parts of the country. This was not enough to allay fears in those parts where high unemployment was, in post-war terms, a novelty but was more than enough to kindle resentment in the assisted areas because the differentials in their favour were being reduced.

In January 1972, the month in which unemployment nationally first topped the million mark, figures were published showing that estimated new jobs during 1971 in the Development and Special Development Areas totalled only 66,000 or 40% below the 1970 figure. The disadvantage of investment allowances over investment grants was also at its maximum at that time as so many firms were earning low profits or none at all. The comparative advantage of assisted areas was further diminished when in his budget a few months later, the Chancellor raised the initial allowances on plant and machinery to 40% throughout the country.

In the Spring of 1972, the government did a U-turn on regional policy almost as complete as the one it was soon to do on incomes policy. The new regional policy was set out in a White Paper (Cmnd 4942), "Industrial and Regional Development", and given legislative effect in August with the passing of the Industry Act. Reliance on tax incentives which was the reason for substituting allowances for grants earlier on, was discarded and a Regional Development Grant instituted. These grants were payable at the rate of 22% in SDAs and 20% in DAs, in respect of plant and machinery and of industrial buildings. Intermediate Areas qualified for the 20% building grant but not for the grant for plant and machinery. A new feature of this Act was that grants were payable to firms already in assisted areas and not just to new firms moving in. Only manufacturing and building firms could qualify.

The government took the opportunity at the time the White Paper was published to make known its revised intentions on the Regional Employment Premium. Instead of terminating it abruptly in September 1974, they would phase it out over a period beginning in that month. They also offered a further easement to firms wanting to set up or expand in DAs or SDAs; they could now do so without having to obtain an industrial development certificate. Finally, Intermediate Area status was extended to more parts of the North West, Yorks and Humberside and Wales. Now nearly half the country's population was living in areas receiving some sort of assistance.

The government's policy was not, however, without its critics. The Trade and Industry Sub-Committee of the House of Commons Expenditure Committee, reporting in December 1973, noted the hit-and-miss manner in which it was applied and called for a more rational and systematic approach to Regional Affairs. There was also a sizeable minority in the Conservative party who viewed the whole idea of government intervention in the location of industry with misgivings; the national interest, they believed, would best be served by letting market forces determine where and what industry should produce. This laissez-faire undercurrent would become mainstream philosophy of the next Conservative government.

Urban Unemployment
One of the major deficiencies in Development Areas was a lack of the service industry jobs which were available in some abundance in other parts of the country, especially London. High office rentals, expensive housing and congested roads, all contributed to the social costs of this maldistribution of office and other service employment. In 1963, the Conservatives had established the Location of Offices Bureau in order to help firms on a purely voluntary basis to site their offices away from the centre of London. Labour felt that something with more bite was needed and in 1965, passed the Control of Office and Industrial Development Act. Under this Act, the building of offices larger than 3,000 square feet in London could only be undertaken if an Office Development Permit was obtained from the Board of Trade.

Later on, similar restrictions on office development were imposed on East Anglia, the Midlands and the rest of the South East. The effect of these measures was at best marginal. Labour shortages in the service industries in some parts of the country continued to co-exist with lack of service jobs in other parts.

London and other large areas also had problems of an opposite sort: enclaves of high unemployment in their midst often occurring, as in London itself, when the surrounding areas were prosperous. This had come about because much of manufacturing industry, which used to be the main job providers in these areas, had closed down or moved elsewhere. With industry had gone many of the young, the more skilled and the more industrious, leaving behind a disproportionate number of the old, the unskilled and the disabled.

The situation was exacerbated, though not caused by, the influx of immigrants from the Caribbean and Afro-Asian countries. Starting as a trickle in the early Fifties, it had swollen to a torrent in the early Sixties. Sadly but inevitably, racial tensions ensued and in 1962, the Conservative government passed an Immigration Act imposing quota restrictions on immigrants from both old and new Commonwealth. In 1965, the Labour government passed a Race Relations Act banning discrimination on grounds of race in public places and establishing a Race Relations Board. In 1968, a further Act was passed extending this coverage to discrimination in employment.

Despite protestations of good will and sympathy, the Labour government no more had an easy answer to the urban problem than they had to the Regional problem. But most of this urban decay occurred in areas which were solidly Labour and they did not want to appear to be leaving these areas to unbenign neglect. Hence the inception in 1968, of the Urban Aid Programme, designed to assist with housing, health and education in all cities with special needs. Though not a job-creating initiative as such, it was designed to ameliorate conditions which were very much interlinked with unemployment. Starting with an allocation of £22 million in its first year of operation the cost soon rose to double that amount.

Continued support for Urban Aid by the Heath government was not a matter greatly to stir the general public and during the period 1970-74, very little was heard about the inner cities. This was partly because the indignities suffered by their unfortunate inhabitants made far less exciting news for the media than the polemics which were raging over the Industrial Relations Act and incomes policy, and partly because, despite the short-lived clamour over unemployment in 1971-72, neither expert nor amateur realised that the era of full employment was drawing to its close.

In the 1950s, it had been generally assumed that full employment and the welfare state had abolished poverty. In the Sixties poverty, it was said, had been "rediscovered" and the Affluent Society was seen to have its "flip" side. Professor Peter Townsend's researches into poverty unearthed facts that had lain hidden for two decades whilst organisations like Shelter, the Low Pay Unit and the Child Poverty Action Group also came into being and did their best to alert and spur to action the rest of the community.

But still the true wretchedness in these urban ghettos went unheeded by the vast mass of comfortably-living citizens and almost unalleviated by a government swamped and distracted by a sea of other troubles.

CHAPTER FOUR
AN IDEAL DEMOLISHED, Feb 1974 - June 1983

The Seven Month Government, Feb 1974 - Sept 1974.

Almost on the very day that Heath announced that he was going to the country, figures were published showing that unemployment had risen from 2.4% to 2.5%. Parliament and public had long grown to regard this level as acceptable and the atmosphere of crisis which characterised virtually the whole period of the 1974 government at no time centred on unemployment. The overriding aim of the new Labour government in February 1974 was to consolidate and improve their standing with voters so that they could call another general election and win a clear majority as soon as possible.

No-one doubted what was their first task, i.e. to settle the miners' dispute and get industry back to normal working. Within a few days of taking office a report on the relativities of miners' pay was received from the Pay Board. This gave the government the rationale it wanted for settling the dispute - never mind the cost - by granting the coal miners pay rises ranging from just over 22% to nearly 32%. By the end of March, the miners were back at work and the State of Emergency was over.

The government were still left facing the formidable consequences of the rise in commodity prices and oil. Economic growth which had reached 6% in 1973, had ground almost to a halt and the balance of payments was once again in the red. More disturbing still was the acceleration in inflation, much of it triggered by the agreement on threshold payments which the Heath government had introduced and which the Wilson government, hoping to go to the country again before long, felt it impolitic as yet to terminate.

Nothing was done during this 7 ½ month Parliament (the shortest in the twentieth century) to tackle the economic problems at source.

Nevertheless, the government could not just let the economic wounds fester without attention. By a marvel of stamina and intellectual potency, Denis Healey, the new Chancellor of the Exchequer, introduced his first budget within three weeks of being appointed. It proved to be a balancing act. Rises in the standard rate of income tax were offset by increases in the personal and child tax allowances; subsidies to the nationalised industries were reduced by about £500 million and food subsidies increased by a similar amount.

Four months later, as industrial production flagged and the gloom of the business world deepened, Healey introduced some mildly reflationary measures. The Regional Employment Premium was doubled, dividend controls were eased and VAT reduced from 10% to 8%.

By this time inflation was running at the rate of 16 1/2% per annum. It was cause for special concern that commodity and oil price rises were now decelerating whilst domestically generated price rises were accelerating. The government's main - though ineffectual - answer was to try and strengthen the Social Contract with the unions.

In August the government issued a White Paper (Cmnd 5710) entitled, 'The Regeneration of British Industry'. In it they set out their plans for modernising British industry and setting it on the expansionary course which had so long defied successive governments. The main instrument for all this was to be a National Enterprise Board with powers to conclude planning agreements with major companies.

Tony Benn, Secretary of State for Industry at that time, and most of the left wing of the Labour party were desperately anxious to make those agreements compulsory. The more pragmatic Wilson, well aware that compulsion would enrage industrialists and alienate many of the middle-of-the-road voters, made sure that when, a year later, they were embodied in legislative form, they provided only for voluntary agreements. (Benn himself was moved in June 1975 from the Department of Industry where he had been anathematised by both employers and press to the Department of Energy, where, so the Prime Minister hoped, the barrage of criticism would fall less heavily and a little further away from the nerve-centre of government.)

The White Paper of August 1974 and the National Plan of 1965 contained similarities both in their origin and in their aborted lives. Both appeared on the scene when Labour was fighting to turn a precarious into a safe majority in Parliament and both failed to set the British economy on the expansionary course hoped for. The NEB, so far from "introducing public ownership into the strongholds of private industry" as intended, was mainly used on rescue operations, for example, British Leyland, Harland and Wolf and Chrysler UK. The only planning agreement reached was the one with Chrysler in December 1975. The government was saved from having to face the embarrassment of having 17,000 Chrysler employees (6,000 of them at their Scottish plant at Linwood) made redundant at a time when unemployment generally was well in excess of a million.

In the weeks before the October 1974 election, unemployment was propelled briefly to the forefront of the political stage, not because of any startling upsurge in the numbers out of work, but because of a speech delivered in Preston in early September by Sir Keith Joseph.

All post-war governments, he told his audience, had been dominated by the fear of unemployment and had fought this unemployment by creating too much money. They had assumed that the resulting inflation would only be mild because mild inflation seemed a painless way of maintaining full employment. That was why "often against their own better judgement" they had tried to spend their way out of unemployment whilst relying on incomes policy to damp down the effects.

Sir Keith then analysed the composition of the unemployment registers in support of his contention that except on a regional scale, there had always been full employment, sometimes "fuller than full employment". On the national rather than the regional scale, the unemployment registers largely consisted of persons on the move from job to job ('frictional unemployment'), the inadequate, the aged, the ill and an unquantifiable proportion of the fraudulent. The government were no longer dealing with "those gaunt, tight-lipped men in cap and mufflers of the 1930s".

"What must be done," he said, "was to set a level of demand sufficient for that level of full employment which could be sustained without inflationary pressures and then to work within it to deal with specific employment problems." This meant that governments should "curb the money supply", the effects of doing which would be "largely temporary". He did not believe that if we got the money supply right everything would be right, but that "if we got the money supply wrong - too high or too low - nothing would come right".

The Times, which had given the speech front page and first leader publicity, referred to it as "an extraordinary political testament" which rejected the whole bi-partisan basis of post-war full employment policies as pursued by governments of both parties. It was: "a root and branch condemnation of the whole economic strategy followed by Mr Heath and Mr Barber from the summer of 1971 to the last election."

The Economist applauded the fresh thinking which Sir Keith had brought to the problems of the day, but noted: "Sir Keith is in some difficulties to explain the present situation with the threat of both mass unemployment (demand deficiency?) and hyper-inflation (excess demand?)...With an incomes policy total real income can be kept up; but the power of the big unions then confronts the government."

With an election in the offing (Wilson announced the election date only thirteen days after Sir Keith had delivered his speech) there was no public censure from the Conservative party leader either of the content of the speech or because the lecture on economic policy had been given by one whose shadow cabinet responsibility was Home Affairs.

There were others in the Shadow Cabinet who felt that Sir Keith had put into words thoughts which had long been latent - none more so than Margaret Thatcher, at that time shadow spokesperson for financial affairs and public expenditure, and within less than six months to be elected Conservative leader. The speech also made a deep impression on many backbenchers. Only with reluctance had they gone along with Heath and his Cabinet when, against their election manifesto and traditional Conservative philosophy, they had introduced a statutory incomes policy and in other ways too had proved themselves more interventionist in industrial affairs than Labour. To them Sir Keith's utterance sounded like the true voice of Conservatism.

However, the full significance of the speech had hardly sunk in before the country was in the throes of an election campaign, polling day having been fixed for 10 October. There was no doubt what was to be the main issue of the campaign, inflation, Labour proclaiming in their manifesto that the battle against inflation was "the first priority", whilst the Conservatives declared in their manifesto, "everything else is secondary". As is usual in such circumstances, each side bandied statistics at each other, carefully selecting their base dates to make them as favourable to their own cause as possible.

Labour's chief weapon against inflation was still the Social Contract. "At the heart of this manifesto," ran their message to the country, "and our programme to save the nation lies the Social Contract between the Labour government and the trade unions."

The Conservatives placed more emphasis on the method of approach than on specifics of what should be done. "The nation's crisis," their manifesto declared, "should transcend party differences; the only way the battle can be won is by the people of this country uniting on a national policy."

What gave the subject of unemployment its topicality was not its current level - 2.5%, but the supposed link between low unemployment and high inflation. This ensured that it would receive more attention from Parliamentary candidates than it had received at the February election. Fifty-two percent of Conservatives and thirty-five percent of Labour candidates whose election addresses were examined by David Butler in his election post-mortem, mentioned unemployment compared with 17% and 16% respectively in February.

The Conservatives noted in their manifesto that unemployment was rising and cited it as one of the three economic dangers facing the country, the other two being inflation and the balance of payments deficit. Like Labour, however, they regarded unemployment as primarily a problem of the regions, undertaking to continue the assistance available under the Industry Act 1972, and promising "continuity of assistance in order to achieve a real breakthrough in solving long-term problems".

Labour were a little more specific in their undertakings to the worst hit of the assisted areas, promising to set up Scottish and Welsh Development Agencies. But they too refrained from offering major reflation as a general cure for unemployment. Their main instrument for making industry more efficient and jobs more plentiful, was to be the establishment of a National Enterprise Board, as mentioned earlier.

With the ordinary voter, what an as yet unborn NEB might or might not do was of small importance compared with what prices might or might not do. As Table 12 opposite shows, rather more voters felt that Labour would do the better job in this respect. The Conservatives' share of the vote fell from 37.9% to 35.8%, whilst Labour's share rose from 37.1% to 39.2%.

Labour now held the overall majority which they had failed to achieve in February, but one of only three. Clearly this exiguous lead would be at hazard to by-election losses, abnormal sickness and unforeseen political set-backs. They would have to take very careful note of the aspirations of Scottish and Welsh nationalists, not to mention the voting intentions of the still cruelly unrepresented Liberals.

Table 12

Gereal Election of 10th October 1974

Party	Votes Received	Percentage Votes	Number of MPs
Labour	11,457,079	39.2	319
Conservatives	10,464,817	35.8	277
Liberals	5,346,754	18.3	13
Northern Ireland	702,094	2.4	12
SNP	839,617	2.9	11
Plaid Cymru	166,321	0.6	3
Others	212,496	0.8	Nil

Unemployment Up to a Million, Oct 1974 - July 1975.

Only the very dedicated or those avid for power could rejoice in the bed of nails which was the new Labour government's inheritance. Both inflation and wage claims were steadily rising, the balance of payments was sliding more deeply into the red and unemployment was creeping up ominously. Repeal of the Industrial Relations Act had allayed but not eliminated industrial unrest.

It was unfortunate, therefore, that so much of the government's time and attention was diverted from those urgent economic matters to the problem of the Common Market. In their manifesto, Labour had committed itself to a "fundamental re-negotiation of the terms of entry" and "to the outcome being submitted to the British people" for final decision. This meant either holding another general election or having a referendum during 1975.

Despite the efforts of Harold Wilson and George Brown to negotiate Britain's entry to the EEC a few years earlier, the majority of the Labour movement were suspicious of the whole operation and at their annual Conference in the autumn of 1971, the party voted by 5 to 1 against entry. Wilson could not fail to take note of such unequivocal advocacy and soon after Britain gained entry under the Conservative government (from 1 January 1973), he gave the undertaking that any future Labour government would negotiate new terms of entry. They would then consult the British people on whether to accept them or pull out (a process which, because of Treaty obligations, might prove very difficult).

Quickly after Labour regained power, George (later Lord) Thomson was appointed to carry out these negotiations. By the middle of March 1975, the process of re-negotiating entry terms was deemed to have been completed, although few observers could detect any significant improvement in them. Nevertheless Harold Wilson felt that he could present them to the nation in a sufficiently favourable light to ensure approval. As another election so soon after the two in 1974 was out of the question, this meant the novel expedient of submitting them to the British people for referendum.

Despite wide and often bitter discussions within both Labour and Conservative parties, each failed to reach agreement in their own ranks and the referendum held on 5 June 1975 ended in 67.2% of those voting saying "Yes" to entry and 38.2% saying "No". Only 64% of the electorate voted.

Meanwhile the rise in prices was gathering momentum, speeded on by the succession of threshold agreements which fell due between their inception in October 1973 and their termination in November 1974. Introducing another budget in the autumn of that year, Healey emphasised that the most disturbing aspect of the situation was that metal and other raw material and oil prices were stable. The conclusion was inescapable that much of Britain's inflation was domestically generated.

These hard realities left little scope for the expansionary measures which on Keynesian principles would have been the reaction to an unemployment level of 2.7%. Almost the only items of relief were £285 million in tax concessions to the elderly and £775 million for industry to offset the effect of inflation on stock valuations.

As well as the calculable difficulties already confronting the government were the hazards of forecasting aptly put by Healey in his Autumn Statement. "The origin of these forecasts," he stated, "lies in the extrapolation from a partially unknown past, through an unknown present, to an unknowable future, according to theories about the causal relationships between certain economic variables which are hotly disputed by academic economists, and may well change from country to country or from decade to decade."

These hazards were well exemplified by Healey's own predictions about unemployment. "Our present forecast," he stated, "which includes the effects of the present budget is that the rise in unemployment will be modest and its level will remain below one million." True, he qualified his remarks by saying that much would depend on the development of the world economic situation. But there is no doubt that (to use his own phraseology) he would have regarded as a "silly-billy" anyone who had forecasted at that time what really happened, i.e. a rise to over a million in eight and over a million and a half in fifteen months time.

In April 1975, he was introducing yet another budget and forecasting an unemployment level very different from what he had forecast five months earlier. Repeating his admonition that inflation was now more domestically than internationally generated, he emphasised the need to restrain wage increases, limit the Public Sector Borrowing Requirement and keep the rate of money expansion well under control. He then outlined measures which would cut public spending by £900 million, reduce food subsidies and increase both direct and indirect taxes. He went on to say, "The effect of the budget measures on employment has given me great concern since I absolutely reject the use of mass unemployment as an instrument of policy and this year employment will be seriously affected in any case by the world recession springing from the oil crisis...With all the necessary precautions I predict that, given a low level of trade in 1975, the pressure of demand in the UK will continue easing and unemployment will continue to rise for the remainder of the year. I warn the House that it could be touching one million by the end of the year."

No serious attempt was made to reverse the unemployment trend, although Healey did propose to allocate an additional £20 million in 1975-76 and £30 million in 1976-77 to the Manpower Services Commission for training and special employment measures.

The interlocking economic pressures reached a climax in the summer of 1975. In June, inflation reached its highest point. On an annual basis prices were up by 26.6% and hourly wage rates by 32%. The lack of confidence in sterling was indicated by the loss of $934 from the UK currency reserves during May and June. On 1 July, Healey announced that the government would in future impose cash (instead of volume) limits on public expenditure, arguing that the reduction in real terms which this would bring, would prove a useful anti-inflationary tool.

Obviously some device with far more bite to it than the Social Contract was needed if it were to have any effect on prices. The Wilson government, like the Heath government before them, now found themselves doing a U-turn on incomes policy. They were doing it, however, in a climate far more favourable to its success in the short term, however precarious it might be over the long term.

The trade union leaders knew in their heart of hearts that the Social Contract had failed, were well aware that a large proportion of the general public blamed the unions for this failure and realised that if high inflation soared to hyper-inflation, their members would suffer together with everyone else. In view of the Labour party's manifesto commitment, repeated on sundry other occasions, that there would be no statutory incomes policy, the atttitude of the trade unions to a policy which would be formal but not statutory was crucial.

The nature of this policy was made known in a White Paper (Cmnd 6151), issued on 11 July 1975 and entitled The Attack on Inflation. The basis of these proposals so far as incomes were concerned was a £6 flat rate limit to pay rises on incomes of £8,500 a year or less - nothing to those earning more than £8,500.

The government had reason to feel both encouraged and apprehensive. It was encouraging that the strongest advocate of the £6 pay rise limit was Jack Jones, General Secretary of the powerful Transport and General Workers Union; this should make it more acceptable to the general mass of workers. Apprehension was justified because it soon became clear that it was unacceptable to a large section of the Labour movement. The General Council of the TUC, meeting almost simultaneously with the publication of the White Paper, voted to accept the £6 limit but the majority was only 19 to 13. Furthermore, when the House of Commons voted on the counter-inflation policy less than a fortnight later, 54 Labour members abstained.

Those straining to detect some ray of hope in those gloomy days might have noted that the first landings of North Sea Oil were now being made. But this was of little consolation either to the government enmeshed in its current difficulties or to the growing army of the unemployed whose number at the July head count exceeded a million.

In Hock to the I.M.F., Aug 1975 - Dec 1976.

On past form with the tally of unemployed up to one million, the government should have pulled out all the stops to get it down again. That is what the Heath government had done even at the price of inflicting severe damage to the economy in other respects. How much more, therefore, might counter-cyclical measures be expected of a Labour government committed by creed to full employment and by doctrine sympathetic to interventionist measures.

Such reckonings would have been wide of the mark. Counter-measures there were both against inflation and unemployment, the former drastic and, in many respects, novel, the latter more an exercise in damage limitation than the sort of reflationary programme by which former governments had tackled (much smaller) rises in unemployment.

All governments expect to be and invariably are criticised by the Press, but the Labour government and Denis Healey in particular, were at this time subjected to a particularly virulent press campaign, the main theme of which was the high level of public expenditure. They were not mollified by the negotiation in January 1976 of a £975 million IMF standby credit. If, it was argued, the economy was in sound health, such borrowings would not be necessary.

The volume of criticism waxed rather than waned after the publication in February 1976 of the annual White Paper on Public Expenditure to 1979-80 (Cmnd 6393). It was not enough, the opposition contended, that public expenditure was programmed to fall in real terms in future years - if, that is, the programme was really adhered to - or that there was to be improved monitoring of such expenditure, plus the imposition over a wide field of expenditure of cash limits.

The opposition campaign was not just fractious; the White Paper itself pointed out that public expenditure in the past three years had grown by nearly 20% whilst the growth in output was less than 2%.

In these circumstances, the government considered that any major expansionary programme to bring down unemployment was out of the question. All they could propose was a few minor palliatives. The first of these related to Community Industry, a scheme started by the Heath government in 1972 to provide work on socially useful projects for disadvantaged youngsters, the aim being to settle them in permanent jobs elsewhere once their Community Industry stint was over. It was announced in August 1975 that the number of places on Community Industry would be expanded to provide 4,000 instead of the current 2,000 places - hardly a torrent of new opportunities! Also announced during August was the Temporary Employment Subsidy (T.E.S.). Under this scheme employers in assisted areas were eligible to receive £20 per week for up to six months in respect of each employee who without this subsidy, would have been made redundant. Some months after its inception it was later extended to cover the country as a whole.

In October, the government announced two more schemes, the Recruitment Subsidy for School Leavers (RSSL) and the Job Creation Programme. Under the RSSL scheme, an employer became entitled to a subsidy of £5 a week for each school leaver he recruited. This scheme was later replaced by the Youth Employment Subsidy under which employers were entitled to £10 per week for every recruit under twenty years of age who had been unemployed for six months or more. More details about these Special Employment Schemes are given later (see page 164). Unease about youth unemployment was fully justified as the table on the following page shows.

At the time Healey introduced his 1976 budget, prices were rising at an annual rate of 19%, an improvement on the 26.6% peak in the previous summer, but still at a level which all parties agreed was intolerable.

An innovatory and controversial feature of this budget was its "conditional clauses". The Chancellor made the introduction of higher tax allowances conditional on the TUC agreeing to limits on wage increases. Negotiations were opened with the trade unions without delay and early in May, the TUC agreed to a policy which it was believed would keep wage awards down to an average of 4.5%.

Table 13

School Leavers in UK not yet in Employment

Oct 1973	5,900
Oct 1974	15,100
Oct 1975	69,600
Oct 1976	82,700
Oct 1977	98,600
Oct 1978	82,000
Oct 1979	69,400
Oct 1980	145,800

Unemployment was by this time well over 1 1/4 million. Commenting on these figures in his budget speech, Healey told the House: "The £6 pay limit has not cured unemployment in Britain. But it has ensured that hundreds of thousands of men and women are now in work who would otherwise have lost their jobs in the inevitable collapse of confidence at home and abroad and in the deflationary measures which would have had to follow."

This modest progress on the inflation front failed to ward off attacks on the pound which, by the end of May, had sunk to $1.76. Believing that by now sterling had been forced down below what was economically justified, the Group of Ten major industrial countries provided Britain in June with a stand-by credit of $5.3 billion which the British government hoped would save them from having to borrow from the IMF with all which that would imply in terms of loss of financial and economic independence.

There was no prospect of the rise in unemployment being stemmed so long as the government pursued its current policies. All the government could bring themselves to do was a little more patchwork. In September, a new scheme, the Work Experience Programme, was introduced. This was designed to provide young persons with a minimum of six months experience in factory, office or shops. Recruits under this scheme were to receive an allowance of £16 a week. The response of employers to this scheme was sluggish.

Quite understandably, a significant portion of the Labour Party found this subordination of employment considerations to other economic aims obnoxious. But Healey stuck bravely - or stubbornly, according to one's point of view - to his policy and in July announced another £1 billion worth of economy cuts for the year 1977-78. Satisfaction by employers that the government did at last seem to be grasping the nettle of soaring public expenditure was largely erased by outrage that he proposed to add a 2% surcharge to the National Insurance contributions payable by employers.

The government's perplexity was graphically exposed to public view in September when Callaghan, who had taken over the Premiership in March, after Harold Wilson's surprise resignation, addressed the Labour Party Conference. In words which seemed to epitomise the penury if not the bankruptcy of government policy, he told the Conference: "We used to think that you could spend your way out of a recession and increase employment by cutting taxes and boosting government spending. I tell you in all candour that that option no longer exists, and in so far as it ever did exist, it worked by injecting inflation into the economy. And each time that happened the average level of unemployment has risen. Higher inflation followed by higher unemployment. This is the history of the last twenty years."

That speech was not the final shame in this worst of all years for the 1974-79 Labour government. On 28 September, television viewers were treated to the spectacle of Denis Healey hurrying back from Heathrow where he was about to board a plane for a meeting of Commonwealth Finance Ministers in Hong Kong to be followed by a meeting of the IMF in Manilla. The reason for this precipitate return was the continued fall of the pound and the belief that it would be folly to squander the unused portion of Britain's $5.3 billion stand-by credit agreed by USA and other financial powers in May in a vain attempt to halt the fall. On the following day, application was made to the IMF for a loan of £3.9 billion.

As many a Third World country could testify, a loan from the IMF involves close surveillance of the borrowing country's economic conduct. The terms to which the British government had agreed to return for the £3.9 billion loan they had requested were set out in a Letter of Intent despatched to the IMF on 15 December 1976.

The Public Sector Borrowing Requirement, which stood at £10.6 million in 1975-76 was to be reduced to £8.6 billion in 1978-79 public spending cuts of £1.5 billion were to be achieved over and above those already planned, whilst the increase in M3 was to be contained between 9% and 13% in the coming year. (M3 is the measurement of money as comprised of coins in circulation and all resident deposits in UK banks in both sterling and foreign currencies).

From about this time can be traced the hostility amongst trade unions and Labour supporters generally to monetarism, which was to rise to a crescendo when it was paraded as a major instrument of policy in the early days of the Thatcher government. To ordinary men and women the process by which it worked seemed mysterious if not sinister, whilst its consequences in redundancies and reduced welfare expenditure were only too evident. Moreover, those with an ear to the international scene had heard horrifying stories of the effects of monetarism as applied by the brutal and unsparing Pinochet regime in Chile.

This antipathy to monetarism did not prevent Healey from making increasing use of monetary methods even if he played down the use of the term.

Bailed Out by the Lib-Lab Pact, Jan 1977 - May 1978

Whilst these economic agonies were being enacted, significant things were happening on the political front. From the beginning of their administration the Labour government's task had been complicated by the presence of 11 SNP (Scottish Nationalists) and 3 Plaid Cymru (Welsh Nationalists) and it was this factor which caused their defeat when they tried to apply the guillotine in a debate on devolution in February 1977. Moreover, by this time they had lost their overall majority due to a succession of by-election defeats. Nor was their task made any easier by the fusillade of criticism from their own disappointed and disgruntled left wing.

On the ropes, perhaps, but they were not yet down for the count and in March their position in Parliament was greatly bolstered by the conclusion of a pact with the Liberals. The thirteen Liberals now under the leadership of David Steel, agreed to support Labour in a vote of confidence in return for a promise that the government would consult them on pending legislation; would introduce legislation for devolution in Scotland and Wales and would hold a free vote in Parliament on proportional representation in the forthcoming elections for a European Parliament. (Proportional representation for European elections was defeated in the House of Commons on 13 December.)

On 23 March, supported now by the Liberals, the government survived a no-confidence vote by 322 votes to 298. Six days after defeat of the no-confidence vote, Healey was back in the House of Commons introducing yet another budget. Since the turn of the year, the economy had shown a remarkable improvement. The exchange rate was now steady at $1.72, reserves at £9.6 billion were double their October low, whilst MLR had come down from 15% to 10 1/2%. At last Healey had something to offer which tax payers would find palatable. Although indirect taxes were increased by £800 million, direct taxes were reduced by £2.25 billion, resulting in a net reduction in taxation of nearly £1.5 billion.

As in 1976, these tax reductions would only become effective in full if the unions agreed to a pay deal. On 15 July, he reported that agreement had been reached with the unions. In fact the only firm undertaking given by the TUC was that they would do their best (they had and have no powers of compulsion) to ensure that a full twelve months elapsed between settlements. On this rather flimsy assurance the government proceeded, with only minor changes, to implement the budget as at first proposed.

No doubt the mass of tax-payers were glad to see their tax burdens lightened rather than weighted down still more. But this belief was too little and too late to be reflected in any early rise in the government's popularity, as was shown by the Ashford by-election on 28 April, in which a Labour majority of nearly 23,000 was turned into a Conservative majority of 264. The anti-government mood of the country was confirmed a week later when the Conservatives made sweeping gains in local elections.

It did not help Labour's fortunes that the slight improvement in the economic situation had not yet wrought any significant change in the unemployment figures.

Although the Conservatives routinely attacked Labour for allowing unemployment to rise so high, the main theme of their assaults was the government's inability to get on top of inflation, which they knew was the principal worry of the general public. Moreover, many of them must have had a shrewd suspicion that the transition to a market economy which Margaret Thatcher and Keith Joseph were constantly preaching, could not be accomplished without at least an initial rise in unemployment.

Labour members too were well aware that until they could get rid of inflation they were walking the political scene with a noose around their necks. But the government still felt unable to mount any general reflation even though not to do so meant acquiescing in an unemployment level deemed to be "intolerable". The limit to which they were prepared to go was to increase the numbers benefiting from what they termed their "Special Schemes" and introduce from early 1977 a new one, the Job Release Scheme. Under this scheme a worker could take retirement a year early so long as his or her employer agreed to recruit a replacement from the unemployment register. But there was still nervousness about unemployment as was shown by the fate of a report on unemployment produced by the Central Policy Review Staff shortly before Christmas 1977. It began by saying that, "if nothing was done", unemployment would reach three million by the early mid-Eighties. This sentence was removed from the final version of the report on the grounds that it might be thought scaremongering or exaggerated.

It went on to examine the argument that concern about high levels of unemployment was unjustified because unemployment and other benefits protected everyone from the extremes of poverty it caused during the Thirties. This argument was dismissed on the grounds that, for the individual, high levels of long-term unemployment led to low morale, boredom, social isolation, feelings of inadequacy and material losses. For the nation it led to waste and inefficiency. Nor were increased leisure, more adult education, earlier retirement and improvement in training opportunities for young persons acceptable alternatives to providing people with work, desirable though all these were in their own right.

Oddly, perhaps, as confidence in conventional Keynesian principles was at that time beginning to wane, it came down firmly on the side of deliberately stimulating the economy by tax reductions, greater public expenditure and special counter-cyclical schemes. Inaction, it argued, would increase the obsolescence of capital stock, lead to a rising pound and further weaken British competitiveness.

The Prime Minister decided not to circulate the report to his Cabinet colleagues.

All this time there was increasing resistance amongst factory and office workers to incomes policy. This was not surprising as during the first two years in which it was operating, many workers had suffered an actual fall in their standard of living. Increasingly, the cry went up from the left that the government had abandoned whatever socialist principles they ever had and were now only concerned to present themselves as more efficient managers of capitalism than the Conservatives. Incomes policy was also alienating and sending into the Conservative camp a substantial portion of the skilled and better-off workers who resented the narrowing of pay differentials which was one of its consequences.

Despite these rumbles of future trouble, by the summer of 1978, the tide of opinion was flowing back to Labour. In June, the rate of inflation fell to 7.4%, the lowest point it was to reach during the course of the Labour government, and earnings were now rising faster than prices. The political pay-off to these economic improvements was a glut of Labour gains in local elections and successful resistance to the SNP challenge at a by-election in Hamilton in May. Although the Liberals had announced their intention to end the Lib-Lab pact at the end of the current Parliamentary session, Labour had more cause to feel pleased with their prospects than at any time since their early days of office.

Labour's Last Catastrophic Months, June 1978 - May 1979.

There was no hint in the summer of 1978 of what a troubled autumn and catastrophic winter the government was fated to endure. Their standing in the country had greatly improved even if their control of Parliament because of the ending of the Lib-Lab pact, was now much more precarious.

The government were well aware that, no matter how successful they might be in dealing with other matters, if there was any significant rise in inflation they were doomed. Having got it down from 28% at its peak to under 8%, they had no intention of letting this happen and, on 21 July, they issued a White Paper (Cmnd 7293) laying down 5% as the guide-line for wage increases.

On this occasion, there was to be none of the reluctant acquiescence of TUC and Labour party which had enabled the previous phases of incomes policy to stick. The TUC in September and the Labour Party Conference in October, both rejected the 5% norm by large majorities. It was whilst the TUC Conference was being held that Callaghan sprang his surprise on the country by announcing (on television) that there would be no election that year. Astonishing though that decision was to almost everyone except Callaghan himself, for a month or two events seemed to justify it. At a by-election in the Berwick and East Lothian constituency in October, Labour increased their majority whilst a Gallup poll taken that month showed Labour leading the Conservatives by 47% to 42%.

However, any lingering hope that the government might be able to make its 5% pay policy stick was killed when, shortly before Christmas, the Ford Motor Company, following several weeks strike action by its employees, granted them a 17% wage increase. Even if the government had wanted to get really tough, "pour encourager les autres", they would have found it hard to do so as the House of Commons voted by 285 to 283 against sanctions on employers breaching the 5% policy.

The settlement at Ford meant double trouble for the government: firstly because it set a bench-mark by which other settlements would be measured; and secondly because it seemed to emphasise the efficacy of the strike weapon in wage bargaining.

After Ford's successful defiance came the flood. Soon after Christmas, petrol tanker drivers and road haulage workers went on strike. These were followed by various employees in the public sector, whose lower paid workers were at the bottom of the earnings league and who felt that unless they too showed their mettle, they would be left even further behind. Uncollected rubbish overflowing into the streets in malodorous profusion became a common sight, whilst the media made sure that it was everywhere known that in some places violent secondary picketing was the order of the day and in others the sick

111

were not being transported and the dead lay unburied.

The alarm and anger felt by a large section of the community was immense, much of it directed against the trade unions, not mitigated by the fact that in some cases they were the holders-back rather than the eggers-on of extreme action.

To calm the situation, as they hoped, the Government appointed a Commission under Professor Clegg to examine the comparability question. The election came before it had time to report and, political advantage, as is the wont at such times, outweighing economic prudence, Mrs Thatcher promised in her election campaign that, if elected, she would honour the Clegg awards.

The action of the strikers was as foolish as it was understandable; foolish because at a time when an election could not be far off, it made a free gift to the Conservatives whose new leader had already shown that any government she headed would be anti-union and would have little interest in or sympathy for the lower-paid. It was understandable because, although they had helped to get a Labour government elected to office, they had gained little or nothing in the way of material benefits - and that was what mattered most at the bottom end of the earnings scale. They simply were not prepared to accept a 5% pay rise limit just because a now discredited government said that that was what they ought to accept.

For the government the 'Winter of Discontent' was a fatal blow. After the strikes they made a show of carrying on, but everyone could see that they were only hobbling along. Further hazards came their way as a result of the devolution vote. Legislation required that at least 40% of the electorate in the territory concerned, must vote before devolution would be implemented. In Wales, the vote taken on 1 March, went overwhelmingly against devolution. Whilst in Scotland, although a large majority of those who voted were in favour of devolution, they did not amount to 40% of the electorate.

The Scottish and Welsh Nationalists no longer had any reason to sustain the Labour party in office and the death blow came to the government on 28 March when they were defeated on a vote of no confidence, the first government to lose office in this manner for fifty years. On the following day, the Prime Minister announced that the election would be held on 3 May.

Early polls showed Labour to be about 10% behind the Conservatives in popular support, a gap formidably difficult but not impossible for them to make good if everything went their way. Both parties listed in their manifesto several objectives which they would pursue if elected, each placing the control of inflation at the top of their list. Unfortunately for Labour, a majority of the public believed that the Conservatives would be more likely than Labour to keep prices down, whilst in view of past experiences, they were highly sceptical of Labour's claim to have reached a "concordat" with the unions.

Unemployment, though subordinate to inflation as an issue, was obviously one which neither party could ignore, as it was running at a level more than twice as high as at any previous post-war election. The treatment of the matter by Labour and by the Conservatives was markedly different.

Labour specified "working for a return to full employment" as a major objective in its own right. Expanding on the matter later in their manifesto, they stated: "We do not accept that individuals whose jobs have disappeared should remain unemployed for periods of time which demoralise them and impoverish their families. We pledge ourselves to the progressive introduction of a scheme which will ensure within the lifetime of the next Parliament that no-one shall be unemployed for more than twelve months without receiving either the offer of a job or retraining."

Implicit in the Conservative manifesto for those able to read between the lines was a realisation that unemployment was no longer the election loser it was previously considered to be. Future governments would be free to pursue other economic objectives and more jobs would arise not as a result of a conscious "full employment policy" but from the greater prosperity of the country as a whole. As the manifesto put it: "Too much emphasis has been placed on attempts to preserve existing jobs. We need to concentrate more on the creation of conditions in which new, more modern, more secure, better paid jobs come into existence. This is the best way of helping the unemployed and those threatened with the loss of their jobs in the future."

Although the incidence of unemployment was geographically very uneven, few Parliamentary candidates felt it was a matter they could keep silent about and according to Butler's analysis of election addresses, it gained mention in those of 86% of Conservatives and 85% of Labour candidates. It also figured in what was probably the most telling pictorial blow of the election. This was a poster showing a long, straggling dole queue with the slogan, Labour Isn't Working.

Table 14

General Election of 3rd May 1979

Party	Votes Received	Percentage Votes	Number of MPs
Conservatives	13,697,690	43.9	339
Labour	11,532,148	36.9	269
Liberals	4,313,259	13.8	11
SNP	504,259	1.6	2
Plaid Cymru	132,544	0.4	2
Others	1,039,563	3.4	12

But there was never any serious doubt about the outcome, the main point of interest being the size of the Conservative majority. As Table 14 opposite shows, when all the votes had been counted, the Conservatives had a lead of 70 over Labour and of 43 overall.

'This Lady's Not for Turning,' May 1979 - Oct 1980

No-one was left in any doubt that the top priority of the new government was to bring inflation down. The conquest of inflation was not regarded as just an end in itself but as the means to establishing an economic climate in which the market mechanism would function with maximum efficiency. As the election had shown, unemployment was no longer the issue it used to be and it was the conviction of senior members of government that "proper jobs", a phrase now much used, could only be created as a sequel to not an accompaniment of falling inflation.

The shape of things to come was clearly foreshadowed in the budget which Geoffrey Howe introduced after barely six weeks of office. Monetary growth, as measured by M3, was to be kept for the rest of the 1979-80 financial year, within the 7% to 11% range rather than the 8% to 12% range set by the Labour government. The PSBR would be reduced by £1 billion to £8.3 billion and Minimum Lending Rate was raised from 12% to 14%. The faith in market forces which elevated monetary control to be the chief instrument of economic policy left no role in logic for continuance of exchange controls and Howe announced that these would be dismantled. (This was done in October.)

Cardinal to the government's supply side philosophy was the conviction that high income taxes were a deterrent to effort and enterprise and should be reduced as quickly as possible. A beginning was made in the budget. The top range of tax was reduced from 83% to 60% and the basic rate from 33% to 30%. The loss of revenue from this source would largely be made good by a rise from 8% to 15% in VAT. This was a bold and many thought a foolhardy measure as it would raise the retail price index by nearly 4% at a time when it was known that the Clegg awards would entail wage and salary increases in the public sector of 20% or more and when the international economy was reeling from the latest OPEC oil rise. (Between October 1978 and June 1979 the spot price of Saudi Light Crude had risen from $12.98 to $35.40 a barrel.)

The budget was also an earnest of the anti-egalitarian bias which would imbue so many of the government's social and economic policies in the future. Whilst it put money into the pockets of those already rich or well-to-do, it worsened the lot of thousands who because of low pay or unemployment, were too poor to benefit from income tax relief but who would have to pay the higher prices for their purchases in the shops.

The Chancellor based his measures for reducing public expenditure on the theme: "Finance must determine expenditure not expenditure finance." The government, he said, would not raise cash limits to cover the inflation which had occurred since the estimates for 1979-80 were originally published; nor would they raise them to cover wage or salary increases in the public sector. The Rate Support Grant for local government would be raised by only £335 million, not enough to cover the increase in expenditure in real terms. There would also be reductions in industrial and employment subsidies. In total, these reductions would amount to about £1 1/2 billion in a full year. The only increase he foresaw was that for defence and pensions.

The lowly role in economic priorities assigned to a reduction in unemployment was made clear in almost the only reference to the subject made by Howe in his whole budget speech: "In today's world, higher prices for oil and petrol are inescapable. So too are the consequences of the inflation which has afflicted us for so long. Until that is controlled some check to the growth of output and employment is inevitable."

The rise in oil prices was bound to cause some increase in unemployment in all industrialised countries, but the rise in UK was made worse by the government's adherence to its monetarist policy, its cut-backs on state involvement in industry and the dismantling of the regulatory bodies set up by Labour. The government argued that their policies, though painful, were necessary in order to set British industry free from the coils in which Labour had entrapped it.

In fact, the anticipated rise in unemployment was longer in coming than expected. This was partly because it is usual both in up-turns and down-turns of the economy, for changes in the unemployment level to occur late in the cycle and partly because of the increase in the number of people on Special Employment Schemes - from 248,000 in March 1980 to 367,000 in September.

The real rise in unemployment began in October. A rise of one decimal point in that month was the start of an increase which would take the total, almost with a break, to more than double the already high level which the Conservatives had inherited from Labour and in head count terms, to well over three million.

Beleaguered as they were by difficulties, some within some outside their own control, the Thatcher-led government made it known that this time there would be no flinching or turning back. Defiantly and publicly, they renounced not only the philosophy and handiwork of their Labour predecessors but also the half-heartedness of the previous Conservative government which had wilted when the winds blew hard.

Mrs Thatcher had several times stressed in opposition that there would be no incomes policy and no printing of money to finance "irresponsible" pay settlements. As good as her word, within less than a fortnight of obtaining office, she had authorised her Industry Secretary, Sir Keith Joseph, to announce that the Pay Board and Prices Commission would both be abolished. In a further instalment of new policies, a consultative document on trade union reform was produced by James Prior. Later announcements revealed that Regional Aid would be cut by £223 million, that British Aerospace would be privatised and that the (profitable) telecommunications section of the Post Office would become a separate corporation. Indicative of the consequences which would ensue from these and other measures, was the warning given by Michael Edwards, Chairman of British Leyland, that thirteen plants would be closed and 25,000 jobs would be lost.

Though there was no repetition of the scenes which took place in the Winter of Discontent, the first winter of Conservative rule was in its way as discordant as its predecessor. The unions were fuming because of the proposed legislation to curb their powers and at their exclusion from all major spheres of consultation; the steel workers were on strike for more pay and fewer redundancies; trouble was obviously brewing at the pits; whilst, in the higher reaches of administration, all members of the National Enterprise Board had resigned, following the decision of Sir Keith Joseph to transfer control of Rolls Royce from the NEB to his own department.

Nor was there anything in the way of a boost forthcoming from Howe's budget in March. Its central theme was not unemployment, but a new concept, the Medium Term Financial Strategy (MFTS), the purpose of which was to reduce inflation by steadily declining monetary growth. The effectiveness of the policy would pivot on whether the government could keep the money supply under strict control. The target range for the 1980-81 financial year, as measured by M3, was the 7% to 11% range reducing to 6% to 10% in 1981-82.

Crucial to the outcome of events was the Public Sector Borrowing Requirement, any overrun of which, it was believed, would seriously endanger attainment of the monetary target. The upshot of the budget was to depress demand at a time of deepening recession, a policy quite at odds with the now discarded Keynesian principles but grimly consistent with the government's chosen method of squeezing out inflation.

118

These were gloomy days for the would-be wage earners and their families who were the human material of these formularies and statistics. All too true was the Treasury comment in the Financial Statement which accompanied the budget: "The implication of this forecast is for a further decline in employment and an increase in unemployment." In April, the head count of unemployed passed the 1 1/2 million mark and, in June at 1,600,000 passed the highest point reached under Labour. In August, it reached two million.

Of course, there were protests both in Parliament and in the country. Shortly before the long recess, the Labour party tabled a motion of no confidence in the government whose economic and social policies were "spreading unemployment, undermining British industry and demoralising the country". The debate had no discernible effect on events.

The country was more shaken by events happening outside Parliament. In April 1980, a riot occurred in Bristol, prototype of several which would take place in large towns in the spring and summer of 1981. The immediate cause of the Bristol riot was a police raid on a café where it was believed that drug-dealing was taking place. But it was generally agreed in the enquiry which followed that the protests would not have been so violent or on such a scale had it not been for the increasing number of young people who were at a loose end because they had no jobs and little chance of getting one.

In July, the Synod of the Church of England, ignoring the strictures of a section of the Conservative Party that they were "dabbling in politics", adopted a report by a working party entitled, "Work and the Future". Politicians, trade unions and management were all criticised for ignoring the unemployed and the clergy themselves were told that they could do more.

Some of the protests were more physical. Radio listeners were startled one summer's evening to hear shouts of anger from a number of unemployed who had broken into the hall where the 'Any Questions?'

programme was being held, to protest about unemployment. Nor was it a cheerful scene which greeted delegates to the Conservative Conference in Brighton that autumn. A vast milling crowd gathered outside the Conference Hotel to impress on those attending the Conference and television viewers everywhere, their hostility to the government, its policies and its leader.

It was enough to cow any government, any Prime Minister. Would there be a U-turn as had happened when the Heath government were in extremis? The Prime Minister left the Conference in no doubt on this point, rallying her listeners with the words, "You turn if you want, this lady's not for turning."

Unemployment Climbs to Three Million, Nov 1980 - Jan 1982.

The winter of 1980-81 was marked by two notable political events, the election of Michael Foot in November to the leadership of the Labour Party and the formation in 1981 of the Social Democratic Party. Though the flowerings were different, both events had their roots in the same soil, the leftward lurch of the British Labour Party.

The modern Labour Party has always prided itself on being a broad church, enclosing in its bounds a miscellany of opinions from extreme left to centre-left. During the period of the 1974-79 Labour government, the left had watched with anguish as the party's leaders clamped on the country policies which were the antithesis of all they believed in; in particular, the left resented the rejection of their Alternative Economic Strategy in favour of a policy of savage deflation and high unemployment. But, out of fear of overturning a boat already rocking, they kept their protests within bounds.

With the defeat of Labour at the 1979 election, these dissatisfied groups felt that it was time to assert their influence, a viewpoint particularly strongly held in the constituency parties and in some sections of the trade union movement. When, therefore, the leadership of the party came up for election following Callaghan's resignation in October 1980, there was strong support for Michael Foot, quintessentially a man of the left, but one who as Cabinet Minister and Deputy Leader of the party, had shown himself able to work harmoniously with its top echelons, whilst still retaining the esteem of most of the rank and file. On a second ballot, he defeated Denis Healey, author and expositor of so much which was anathema to the left, by 139 to 129.

As time was to show, the election of Foot as party leader, though explicable in terms of internal Labour politics, was disastrous for the party at the next general election. Amongst other consequences, it doubled the certainty that a second term of office would be accorded to a party to whom full employment was now no longer a specially high priority.

The accession of Foot to the party leadership gave impetus to but did not originate the break-away from the party of three ex-Cabinet Ministers and about a score of back-bench MPs. The policies adopted at Labour's autumn conference had left these dissidents estranged on defence, the future of incomes policy, Britain's continuance in the EEC and the constitutional changes within the Labour Party itself which would have the effect of taking power from the Parliamentary party and giving it to the constituency parties and the trade unions.

It so happened that in January 1981, Roy Jenkins, at one time Deputy Leader of the Labour Party and heir apparent to Harold Wilson, concluded his spell as President of the European Commission at Brussels and was free to join "the rebels". This he promptly did and the Gang of Three (Shirley Williams, David Owen and William Rogers) became the Gang of Four. In March, the Social Democratic Party was formally launched and in June, a political and electoral pact was made with the Liberals.

There was now a third force in being whose aim was to break the mould of British politics by forming a centre-left partnership, purged of what they regarded as the loony left, acknowledging the importance of the market as an economic determinant but more dedicated to social reform and betterment than the "uncaring Tories".

Massive speculation followed as to whether this really did herald the break-up of the two party system with its confrontational absurdities and injustices or whether it was just the gyrations of deviants destined as other rebels had been before them to be laid low by the all-powerful party machines of the two major political contestants.

Whilst these political maneouvrings were taking place, unemployment continued its upward course, reaching 2 1/2 million in April. Any hope that a few "real jobs" might result from the budget were quickly dashed when Howe presented his proposals to the House on 10 March. Total expenditure, he said, would rise by 10% over the previous year largely because of increased payments for unemployment benefit and defence. To meet this expenditure, alcohol and tobacco duties were raised, petrol duties increased and car licences lifted to £100.

What the Chancellor made clear was that the Medium Term Financial Strategy was still the lodestar by which the government would be guided. The monetary target was set within the 6% to 10% range, the same as in the previous year, with a Public Sector Borrowing Requirement of £10.5 billion. This was £3 billion less than the previous year's actual out-turn which had exceeded target by £5 billion.

Ritual regrets were voiced by the Chancellor about unemployment which was an "affront to personal self-respect" and "a waste of human resources". But, he warned, the inflationary policies by which previous governments had tried to tackle the problem were detrimental to employment prospects in the long run. He illustrated his point by reference to British Steel where a prolonged strike in 1980 against redundancies had availed the strikers nothing. "Had painful decisions," he stated, "not been put off in the Seventies, the Corporation would now be in better shape to weather the current slump in demand for steel and far fewer jobs would have been lost."

This harsh budget, imposed at a time when bankruptcies and redundancies were reaching record levels, was judged by a few critics to be courageous and in industry's long-term interests; far more considered it to be foolhardy as well as stony-hearted.

Thatcherism, which was the term now generally used to define the Conservative government's policies, had some staunch supporters in the academic world, but they were a minority. More representative of academic thought was the memorandum signed by 364 economists and published just three weeks after the budget. In it they stated: "There is no basis in economic theory or supporting evidence for the government's belief that by deflating demand they will bring inflation permanently under control and thereby induce an automatic recovery in output and employment. Present policies will deepen the depression, erode the industrial base of our economy and threaten its social and political stability. There are alternative policies and the time has come to reject monetarist policies and consider earnestly which alternative offers the best hope of sustained recovery."

Neither Mrs Thatcher nor her government were unnerved by such a show of agreement in a profession not noted for its intellectual concord. They still held firmly to the view that a genuine improvement in the employment situation would only come about by the defeat of inflation, something which would be achieved by control of the money supply, appropriate interest rates, and containment of wage increases. Formal wage policies had proved abortive in the past but the government could still influence events by direct action on public sector pay, cash limits on local authorities and nationalised industries and the threat of unemployment if the unions were too uppish in the private sector.

During 1980 unemployment had increased by 65% in UK, 26% in West Germany, 13% in France and 4% in Italy, and in 1981, it continued to mount more rapidly in UK than in most other countries.

Four reasons explain this extra rise in UK. First, the governments over-reliance on monetary policy. Secondly, misinterpretation of the signals being sent out by M3. As was realised, its failure to keep within the bounds set for it (7 1/2% to 11% target, 19.4% out-turn in 1980-81) was due not to expansion in money available for general spending but to removal of the monetary corset in June 1980 and distress borrowing by firms trying to avoid bankruptcy. Thirdly, the notorious overmanning in British industry, which meant that it had to do more slimming than its competitors to get on equal terms with them.

A fourth and paradoxical reason was the long-awaited arrival in profusion of North Sea oil. For years the country had been led to believe that once this oil came on stream, it would solve the balance of payments problem and clear the last obstacle holding up economic growth. What happened was that sterling, for so long a weak currency, became a highly desirable one. The exchange value of the pound shot up from $2 when the Conservatives gained office to $2.45 at the end of 1980. British manufacturers found that the rise in export prices which resulted, erected barriers in many markets which it was almost impossible to surmount. Many people felt that this bonanza from oil would have been better used if it had been invested directly in British industry rather than despatched to anywhere in the world where dividends were expected to be high.

By 1981, even in the hitherto prosperous parts of the country, enclaves of poverty and unemployment were now too large to be ignored, whilst in those parts which even at the best of times had never enjoyed more than a morsel of the national prosperity, there was little to keep hope even flickering.

The attention of the country, indeed of the world, was briefly riveted on these areas by an outbreak of serious rioting in London (Brixton) in April, in Manchester (Moss Side) and in Liverpool (Toxteth) in July. The government could not just shrug its shoulders at happenings like this, however determined they were not to abandon their policies in a moment of panic. Lord Justice Scarman was appointed to investigate and report on the disturbances, whilst Michael Heseltine, Secretary of State for the Environment, was despatched to Liverpool to try and bring practical help to Toxteth and the neighbouring areas of deprivation.

In May, the TUC organised a March for Jobs. The event started with 500 marchers who set out from Liverpool on 1 May and ended with a rally of 100,000 in Trafalgar Square on 31 May. They received little comfort from the government. Employment Secretary, James Prior, told them that it would be quite wrong to suggest that the present tragically high level of unemployment was the fault of the present government. However, the March had focused the attention of the nation and, he hoped, that one effect would be to unite the country in a determination to overcome the deep-seated economic problems that had been pulling the nation down for so long. Hardly balm for the wounds of joblessness!

With so much ruin about them - and time speeding them on towards the second half of their electoral term - the government tried to engineer a fall in interest rates. Minimum Lending Rate was cut from 14% to 12%. It was not only British financiers who reacted to this. A substantial flight out of sterling began and by the end of August, the pound had fallen to $1.75. Minimum Lending Rate was moved back to 14% in September and 16% in October. The situation in the money markets stabilised from then on.

In September, Mrs Thatcher carried out a Cabinet reshuffle designed to reduce the number of 'wets' in the Cabinet and increase the number of Ministers in tune with her way of thinking (who were "one of us"!). Norman Tebbit, whose views on economic policy accorded closely to those of Mrs Thatcher, replaced the more consensual James Prior as Secretary of State for Employment.

At the time Tebbit took over his new job there were still 270,000 school leavers on the unemployment registers or 63,000 more than at the same period of the previous year. Adult unemployment in that period had gone up by 876,000.

Towards the end of the year the rise in unemployment became less sharp. But it did not stop and in January 1982, for the first time in British history, the official unemployment figure was in excess of three million.

Labour Trounced, Feb 1982 - May 1983.

There was nothing in the early months of 1982 to indicate the transformation in Conservative party fortunes which would occur before the year was out. Unemployment continued to rise even after the three million mark was passed, whilst the budget which Howe introduced in March, though less punitive than earlier ones, was not the sort to enthuse the general public or put much heart into the party faithful. A wider definition of money than that used in earlier budgets was adopted and the 1982-83 monetary target was set to fall to within the 8% to 12% range, instead of the earlier 5% to 9%. The PSBR was raised from 2.5% to 3.5%.

Of more interest to the man in the street was the regressive changes in taxation. As in previous Howe budgets, those already well-to-do benefited by a fall in direct taxation whilst those too poor to pay income tax were made worse off by an increase of £1 billion in indirect taxation.

How low Conservative fortunes had sunk was indicated by a poll taken shortly after the budget which showed support for the main parties to be standing at Conservatives 31%, Labour 33% and the Alliance 33%. Yet a similar poll taken in July gave a return of 45% for Conservatives, 26% for Labour and 26% for the Alliance.

Two things had happened to cause this turnaround. The first was the Falklands war which, like some 'deus ex machina' in the ancient plays, had erupted on the scene out of the blue. Mrs Thatcher's resolute handling of the situation pleased both serious-minded opponents of military aggression and the mindless jingoists who always bubble up on such occasions.

The second factor was the modest but discernible improvement in the economy. By April 1982 inflation had at last fallen to single figures and by the end of the year was down to 5.4%. It was also important in shaping the mood of the workers that average earnings were now rising faster than the retail price index. Even manufacturing industry was beginning to see some chinks of light. The international recession was starting to lift, bringing improved prospects for British exports. Moreover, it was becoming apparent that in the grim years just behind them, British industry or those sections of British industry which had survived the purges of those years, had reduced their labour forces so drastically that their labour productivity was now much more on a par with their competitors.

1982 was also a year of industrial peace in so far as such peace can be measured in days lost by strike action. For the first time since 1963 the total of days thus lost was below two million. This passivity was due in part to the pounding the unions had received from legislative curbs on their organisation and activities and partly because workers were too scared of losing their jobs to take action which their employers might regard as provocative.

Industrial peace and the glow of victory in the Falklands War gave momentum to the shift of opinion towards the Conservative cause, a shift which gained impetus from the continual dissension in Labour ranks. These divisions within the Labour party gave the government a freedom of action seldom enjoyed by a government in the second half of its term of office.

In no matter was this governmental immunity more manifest than in the unemployment figures. Although the speed of increase was slowing down, the trend was still upwards. In seasonally adjusted terms, it rose from 10.9% at the beginning to 12.4% at the end of the year.

The monthly unemployment count was not the only statistical evidence of the rise in unemployment in the early Eighties. Subsequently published figures showed the number of "confirmed" redundancies which had occurred since 1977. These are given in Table 15 below.

These figures of "confirmed" redundancies differ slightly from actual redundancies as they only cover redundancies "confirmed" (by employers) as "due to occur". Sometimes they never happened or occurred in smaller numbers than expected. Moreover, Section 100 of the Employment Protection Act 1975, which made notifications of impending redundancies mandatory, applied only to redundancies of ten or more employees. However, they do give some idea of the tornado which hit British industry in the early Eighties and the gush of unemployment which followed.

Table 15
Confirmed Redundancies - Great Britain

1977	158,360
1978	172,563
1979	186,784
1980	493,766
1981	532,030
1982	398,006
1983	311,436

Source: Department of Employment Gazette

In place of the moribund consensus that governments should steer the economy along the paths of full employment, there was a shared perplexity concerning what should be done about it, as was evident in Howe's budget speech of March 1982. "For years," he told the House: "it has been argued - it is still argued today - that we could get unemployment down if only we were less concerned to fight inflation. The right dose of reflation, more generous public spending, so the argument runs, would soon see unemployment tumbling down.

Would that it were so easy. But successive governments for twenty years have been tempted to act on that advice. And with what result? All the time the tide has been rising from one business cycle to the next. The truth is that reflation does not create jobs that last. In the longer run it helps to destroy them."

Compare these words with those quoted earlier and repeated here, of James Callaghan to the Labour Party Conference in 1976. "We used to think that you could spend your way out of a recession and increase employment by cutting taxes and boosting government spending. I tell you in all candour that that option no longer exists and in so far as it ever did exist, it worked by injecting inflation into the economy. And each time that happened, the average level of unemployment has risen. Higher inflation followed by higher unemployment. This is the history of the last twenty years."

Although public opinion polls taken at that time supported the government view that the ending of inflation was more important than the reduction of unemployment, there was widespread concern about the prevalence of unemployment amongst young people.

To this the government felt they had a good answer. Shortly before Christmas 1981, they had published a White Paper (Cmnd 8455) accepting in principle proposals for training worked out by the Manpower Services Commission. In the following summer Norman Tebbitt, Secretary of State for Employment, announced that the government had given the go-ahead for a £1 billion Youth Training Scheme to start in September 1983. It would bring together 460,000 employed and unemployed young people under a single integrated scheme to help them acquire the skills they needed to obtain and retain jobs. The guarantee of a place in a training scheme would apply to all unemployed sixteen year-olds.

It seemed to some Conservatives that these proposals would "wrap up" unemployment as an electoral hazard and, as the party was now on strong ground as far as inflation was concerned, they should go to the country in October 1982. Mrs Thatcher was more cautious, which meant in practical terms that she would wait until after the 1983 budget and the local elections.

Unemployment was still well above three million on 15 March, when Howe introduced his last budget. Although the output increase in 1982 at 0.5% had been disappointing, the circumstances were far more favourable for a lenient budget than at the time of any of his previous ones. Largely because of windfall profits from North Sea oil, the estimated PSBR for 1982-83 amounted to only £7.5 billion or £2 billion below forecast. It was raised to £8.2 billion for 1983-84. The greater revenue expected to be available was used, as in his previous budgets, to lower direct taxes. Excise duties and other indirect taxes were raised roughly in line with inflation.

Seven weeks later, the local elections were held. The results, though far from a Conservative landslide, were reassuring enough to clinch the matter. On 9 May, Mrs Thatcher announced that a general election would be held on 9 June.

One piece of luck this (so far) lucky Prime Minister already had under her belt. The Boundary Commission had recently completed its review of constituency boundaries and its findings (having survived litigation by the Labour party) was estimated to be worth thirty seats to the Conservatives.

For the first time since the 1930s, a third force, the Alliance, was a serious contender. If hopes of gaining more votes than either of the other two contenders were fanciful prospects of holding the balance between the two major parties were real enough. Early opinion polls gave the Alliance slightly under, later polls slightly over, 20% support.

However, there were no tremors in the Conservative ranks (a party which once trembled when unemployment exceeded half a million) at going to the polls with an official unemployment total of over three million. Nevertheless, it still vied with inflation (now nicely down to 4%) as a major electoral issue, David Butler's survey of candidates' Addresses showing that 88% of Conservative, 95% of SDP, 98% of Liberal and 100% of labour candidates mentioned unemployment. On inflation the figures were 91%, 66%, 62% and 36% respectively.

If there was a dominant theme, it was which party could best be trusted to run the economy efficiently. Here Mrs Thatcher cut a more impressive figure than Michael Foot, who could arouse wild enthusiasm amongst those already committed to the Labour cause, but left the all-important floating voter unimpressed. Nor did it help the Labour party that their manifesto went out unpolished in style, unrevised in content, with a defence policy which was bound to prove a vote-loser and proposals on the control of inflation which scarcely anyone believed would prove effective. This must surely explain why so few Labour candidates mentioned inflation in their election Addresses. Peter Shore aptly described the manifesto as "the largest suicide note in history".

No party proffered any original or revolutionary remedy for unemployment. Unambitious is perhaps the best way to describe the programmes of all main parties. The Conservatives promised that so long as it remained high they would persevere with their Special Measures, providing help to the long-term unemployed through the Community Programme and for the elderly through early retirement.

Labour proclaimed that getting Britain back to work was a major priority. Their central aim was to reduce unemployment to below one million within five years of taking office. Co-operation with other governments, "especially socialist governments" and "partnership with the unions" would both play a crucial role in achieving this objective.

After past experiences one wonders how many voters were won, how many were lost, by this promise of "partnership with the unions".

The Alliance proposed a "carefully devised and costed job programme" aimed at reducing unemployment by one million within two years. The young would benefit by the extension of the Youth Training Scheme to all sixteen and seventeen year olds, whilst jobs for the long-term unemployed would be provided by a programme of housing and environmental improvements, extension of the Community Programme and expansion of the Social Services.

If there were any doubts about the outcome before the date of polling was announced, they were soon dispelled once campaigning started. All opinion polls showed the gap between Conservative and Labour support to be slowly but decisively widening. Support for the Alliance rose steadily but not quite enough to overtake Labour.

It is difficult to see how any party in British politics can gain victory without gaining the middle ground. "Our aim," the Labour manifesto had stated, "is nothing less than to bring about a fundamental and irreversible shift in the balance of power and wealth in favour of working people and their families." Whatever merits such equalitarian sentiments may have had in terms of abstract justice, they were bound to alarm more voters on this vital middle ground than they reassured.

Although, as Table 16 below shows, the Conservatives increased their overall lead from 43 to 144, their victory was much less overwhelming than these figures might suggest. Votes cast in their favour were lower than in 1979 by nearly 700,000, whilst their percentage of votes cast fell from 43.9% to 42.4%. It was the split opposition vote which landed the other major contenders in the ditch together and the iniquity of the "first past the post" system which denied the Alliance (25.4% of the votes, 3.5% of the seats) of even a tithe of the Parliamentary representation they had earned.

The fact that for nine months the unemployment figures, even on the somewhat questionable basis on which they were now being calculated, had exceeded three million, did not deter voters from sending back to office the government which had been in charge whilst this was happening.

Table 16

General Election of 9th June 1983

Party	Votes Received	Percentage Votes	Number of MPs
Conservatives	13,012,602	42.4	397
Labour	8,457,124	27.6	209
Alliance	7,780,587	25.4	23
SNP	331,975	1.1	2
Plaid Cymru	125,309	0.4	2
Others	968,308	3.1	17

Had Labour or the Lib-Labs jointly defeated the Conservative government unemployment would have been cited as a cause, perhaps a major cause, of the Conservative defeat. The ideal of Full Employment would have been resuscitated and breathing even if not as hale and hearty as a generation ago. As it was the Conservatives could now, in their minds if not with their tongues, dismiss it as an oddity of history only realised for a few brief decades after the war because of the unique circumstances of the times. There was no longer room for such sentimentality in a country in which market forces would determine the ebb and flow of prosperity and in which no price was too high if it helped to get rid of inflation.

Regional and Urban Unemployment, 1974-83.
Regional Unemployment.

When Labour wrested power from the Conservatives in February 1974, it was reasonable to believe that what was needed in the deprived areas was the medicine as before, but in stronger doses and perhaps with different labelling. True, the policy of bringing work to the workers and bestowing various subsidies to firms already in situ had not worked miracles, but it had at least saved them from total catastrophe. Moreover, with unemployment still only at 2.5%, one might have expected that a number of firms would welcome the prospect of stepping free from the congestion and labour shortages of the South and Midlands and moving to where labour was plentiful and where, despite the grim visage of some industrial locations, there was fine scenery and uncluttered countryside nearby.

In their February and October manifestos the Labour party had promised the Regions that they would set up new Planning Machinery, establish Scottish and Welsh Development Agencies, encourage new public enterprise and retain and improve the Regional Employment Premium.

In planning matters the government reinforced the roles of the Regional Economic Planning Councils and Boards by augmenting the staff and enhancing the powers of the Regional Offices of the Department of Trade and Industry; they were now given power to deal with applications under the 1972 Industry Act up to £1 million. (The Labour government never made any bones about the fact that the Conservatives' 1972 Industry Act greatly enhanced the government's powers to intervene in industrial matters as and when they saw fit.)

Scottish and Welsh Development Agencies were set·up in December 1975 and January 1976 respectively. These were empowered to build advance factories, undertake infrastructure improvements and other environmental projects and assist industry through loans and equity capital. Some of the English Regions with Development Areas within their own boundaries resented the favouritism shown to Scotland and Wales and felt that they should receive a similar degree of autonomy and attention.

The government also in their early years followed sterner criteria so far as industrial development certificates were concerned, lowering the limits beyond which a certificate would be required to 5,000 square feet in the South East, 10,000 square feet in other non-assisted areas and 15,000 square feet for Intermediate Areas. Although the I.D.C. requirements remained in force till the end of the 1974-79 Labour government's term of office, it was applied with ever lessening severity as unemployment rose to disturbing heights even in areas which were previously regarded as having a satisfactory volume and variety of jobs.

Nothing better exemplifies how swift was the decline in economic performance and prospects than the government's reversal in REP policy. Having promised in their February 1974 manifesto to "retain and improve" the Regional Employment Premium, they claimed credit in their October manifesto for having more than fulfilled their pledge by doubling the premium a few months after taking office. Yet in July 1976, the rate was reduced and in December of the same year it was abolished altogether. It is true that abolition might have become unavoidable in any case as it was held by the EEC to run foul of Community regulations, but it is doubtful if its demise would have been quite so swift had it not been for the adverse economic conditions of that year.

No previous enactment since the war caused so much consternation in the assisted areas as this one. Employers, especially those in Scotland, felt that the government were robbing them of their greatest advantage over the rest of the country. Moore, Sharples and Tyler, in their study of Regional policies in the Seventies, reckoned that it cost the assisted areas the loss of some 80,000 jobs. Some felt that the government was leading the country back to the 1930s.

This would be an unjustifiably harsh judgement since the 1974-79 government were faced with three difficulties which, though operative before, had never weighed down on them quite as heavily. First was the accelerating trend nationally from manufacturing to service industry jobs. (Between 1971 and 1984 service industry employees increased from 53% to 65% of all employees.) Secondly, due to the upsurge of unemployment on a national scale, previously prosperous regions, especially the West Midlands, were anxious to attract any footloose industrialists looking for a new location. Thirdly, expansion in manufacturing no longer - as in the old days - meant taking on more "hands"; it often meant exactly the reverse as the essence of technological advance is that machines will do the jobs previously done by men or women.

Moreover, the public attitude towards unemployment was beginning to change. The belief was waning that governments could spend their way to full employment without causing intolerable inflation; people were learning to "live with it" - especially if it was someone else's unemployment.

In the days of full employment there was always the hope that the prosperity of the rest of the country would communicate itself to the less fortunate regions. During the second half of the Seventies that hope dwindled to extinction.

Indeed, a resident in the assisted areas looking for encouraging signs in the summer of 1979 would have had difficulty in finding any. A government had just been elected which was avowedly less keen than its Labour predecessors on pouring public money into the high unemployment regions; there was a feeling that public concern was transferring itself from the troubled regions to the troubled cities; and the recent rise in OPEC oil prices foreshadowed the advent of a national and international recession. Furthermore, the monetarist creed to which the new government was dedicated, frowned on the diversion of investment from areas where it was genuinely profitable to areas where it only seemed to be so because of the opiate of public subsidy.

But even a government as enamoured with the beneficence of market forces as the Thatcher government, could not abolish all regional aid at one fell swoop. However, they did not delay in making it clear that cut-backs would be the order of the day. Within a few weeks of assuming office, they announced that regional aid would be reduced from its current annual rate of £603 million to £376 million in 1982-83; also Regional Development Grants would be reduced from 20% to 15% in Development Areas and abolished altogether in Intermediate Areas.

In the same period, the spread of areas eligible to receive regional aid would be concentrated so that the population covered would fall from 40% to 27.5% of the whole country.

Abolished too were the industrial development certificate system and Regional Planning Councils with their Boards. These Councils with their composition of employers, trade unionists and local "worthies" were shining examples of the sort of consensus politics that Mrs Thatcher so much scorned. Although such scorn might be hurtful to those who had put time and effort into making them effective, there is very little evidence that the community as a whole either gained or lost when they disappeared.

Despite the government's free market predilections there were times when political considerations over-ruled ideology and action was taken very much in line with what previous governments had done. A notable example was the announcement in June 1980 by Sir Keith Joseph, Industry Secretary, that in order to alleviate the unemployment caused by steel closures, Port Talbot, Newport and Scunthorpe would all be granted Special Development Area status. The government would also make available £19 million for factory building at Grimsby and Scunthorpe and £10 million for derelict land closure.

Although there were job losses over the whole field of employment, they were particularly high in those regions with a large manufacturing and mining component in their industrial structure. In Wales, losses in the coalmining industry which had been going on for more than a decade, accelerated during the Eighties, whilst the steel industry in the years 1980-82 suffered, according to the Select Committee on

Welsh affairs, losses "never encountered before in a relatively small geographical area". Very little could be done by private investment to revive these industries, whilst the government were unwilling to breach their market economy tenets to the extent of making any substantial injection of public funds into them. The establishment of the Business Statistics Office in Newport and the Driver and Vehicle Licensing Authority in Swansea did little either geographically or occupationally to make good the losses incurred elsewhere in Wales. Similarly, although the Welsh Development Agency sponsored the starting of a number of high technology plants, these were mainly capital intensive undertakings helping if they were successful to boost the wealth producing capability of Wales but making practically no contribution to her unemployment problem.

By many measures, share of the United Kingdom's GDP, reduced immigration, disposable income per head, the 1970s were years of progress for Scotland. But this did not show itself in terms of employment. Moreover, with the increasing importance of the EEC in Britain's economic life, there was growing fear that her geographical location at the perimeter of the Community would work to her detriment. Nevertheless, North Sea oil, coming so conveniently on full stream just as the Conservatives were entering office, presented Scotland with a material bounty. Her old staple industries, iron and steel, ship-building and heavy engineering, continued to shrink to the inevitable detriment of the population dependent on them. Like its Welsh counterpart, the Scottish Development Agency met with a measure of success in trying to establish high technology industries, especially electronics - but with little effect on the overall employment situation.

For many years before 1979, the North of England had been accustomed but not reconciled to being the English region with the highest level of unemployment. This uncoveted lead widened during the recession which followed the 1979 oil price rise. Between 1979 and 1982, the manufacturing labour force was reduced by 22%, i.e. by 90,000 jobs. As in Wales and Scotland, its industrial structure, based on coalmining (already contracting), shipbuilding and heavy engineering, was ill-fitted to the modern world. Its industrial structure was unfortunate in another respect. More employees than in any other region worked in large establishments. In 1981, 37.2% of its workforce were in units exceeding a thousand, compared with a national average of 28.7%. Consequently, when closures or major redundancies occurred, they often impinged with devastating effects on local communities. A sad example was the closure of the steel works at Consett in 1981 making 4,500 workers redundant.

Despite valiant efforts by local individuals and organisations, the economic and doctrinal climate was against any real recovery of industrial health. The North with 16.5% unemployed were still at the top of the unemployment league when votes were being cast at the 1983 general election.

No region suffered so severely from the contraction in manufacturing as the West Midlands, nouveau poor amongst the Regions. During the Fifties and early Sixties, its manufacturing base of vehicles, metal manufacture and engineering, had stood it in good stead and there had been times when it had the lowest unemployment rate in the country. But in the Seventies, failure to keep up with international competition began to take its toll. The recession of the early Eighties accelerated this decline and by June 1983, only the North and Wales (by one decimal point) had higher unemployment rates than the West Midlands. Hardest hit of all was the Metropolitan County of the West Midlands, where between 1978 and 1983 the unemployment rate trebled, reflecting the loss of 225,000 jobs.

Three other factors made the situation in the Regions worse than it would otherwise have been. The first was the notorious overmanning of much of British industry which necessitated on efficiency grounds alone labour force reductions over and above those resulting from the recession. Secondly, was the misjudgment of the British government which induced them to deflate more drastically than other countries and more than the domestic situation required. The third factor was that concern about unemployment both among the general public and in Westminster and Whitehall was being focussed more on its repercussions on the inner cities than in the half-forgotten Labour-voting Regions.

Urban Unemployment.

The main cause of urban unemployment was job losses from manufacturing industry, some of which had gone under due to old-fashioned plant and old-fashioned methods, and some of which had simply migrated to better sites. The result was that many of the younger, more skilled and more vigorous residents had left the inner cities to work elsewhere in new manufacturing industry or in the expanding service industries. Left behind was a residue of elderly or unskilled younger men and women, greatly exceeding in number the amount of suitable jobs likely to become available.

In August 1976, disturbances in Notting Hill convinced the government that greater priority must be given to these enclaves with their baffling and explosive medley of problems.

Early the next year, in a reversal of the policy which had held for many years, the government began to relax the physical controls on office development in inner city areas whilst the Location of Offices Bureau which had been established to encourage the movement of office jobs out of London, was now instructed to do the opposite.

Formal admission that old policies must be reversed was contained in the White Paper, A Policy for the Inner Cities, (Cmnd 6845). The White Paper was followed early in 1978 by the Inner Urban Areas Act.

Under this Act, seven Inner Urban Partnership Areas and twenty-three Programme Authorities were designated, the former having special priority, but both qualifying for financial and other forms of help beyond what was available elsewhere. Areas not included in the priority list could, however, apply for government assistance under the Urban Programme which the former Labour government had introduced in 1968 and which was not abolished when the Inner Urban Areas Act was passed.

Assistance to priority areas took the form of help in land clearance and other measures to improve the local infra-structure, the provision of advice and training and the establishment of facilities for deprived social and ethnic groups.

Early in their administration the Conservative government let it be known that although they would retain existing legislation such as the Inner Urban Areas Act, they would encourage private investors rather than government to revive these areas.

Attempting to put precept into practice, Howe announced in his budget speech of march 1980 that the government proposed to set up Enterprise Zones. Firms settling in these zones would receive 100% capital allowances for commercial and industrial buildings; would be exempt from paying rates or taxes; would cease to be subject to Industrial Training Board regulations and would only have to deliver to government a bare minimum of statistical or other information. It was hoped that, released in this way from red tape and bureaucracy, private industry would move in and revivify these areas.

Initially, eleven such areas were designated and by the end of 1983 a further thirteen had been scheduled. It has been estimated that in the financial years 1981-82 and 1982-83, about 770 new or relocated firms settled in the eleven zones first nominated, creating nearly 8,000 jobs. The snag was that these jobs were very often diverted from other areas and were not additional to those which would have been created had such zones not existed. Furthermore, a high proportion of the undertakings moving in were engaged in activities like warehousing, whose labour demands were small, or engineering which required skills not easily found in the local labour force. There was also a certain amount of antagonism in contiguous areas to these islets of privilege where it was felt that job gains in the Enterprise Zones were job losses elsewhere.

That the plight of the inner cities was something which even a laissez-faire government would have to take seriously was indicated dramatically by the riots which took place in Bristol in April 1980 and in various towns and cities in the summer of 1981, the most serious being in Brixton (London), Toxteth (Liverpool) and Moss Side (Manchester).

The reaction of the government was twofold. Lord Justice Scarman was asked to enquire urgently into the causes of the riots and Michael Heseltine, at that time Environmental Secretary, was despatched on a fact-finding mission to Merseyside where anti-government feeling and unemployment were both amongst the highest in the country.

In his report, Lord Scarman emphasised the link between unemployment and crime, quoting what he had been told at one of the Youth and Community Centres he visited. , "Young people around in the streets all day, with nothing to do and nowhere to go, get together in groups and the 'successful criminal' has a story to tell. So one evil has bred another and as unemployment has grown, in both older and younger generations, crime has become more commonplace and more acceptable. This is a vicious circle to which there is no present end in sight."

Lord Scarman went on to emphasise the stark employment prospects which faced white as well as black youngsters, but felt it was clear that they bore particularly heavily on the blacks. Poor housing was another major source of unrest and blacks believed that they were discriminated against in respect of jobs and housing. No direct action was taken as a result of the Scarman Report (Cmnd 8427), but it remained as a source and reference point for those inside and outside government who were concerned with the problem of the inner cities.

Michael Heseltine spent two weeks in Merseyside and after reporting back to the Cabinet, was given the commission to head a Task Force for the area, comprising civil servants from several government departments and seconded persons of managerial rank from the private sector. It was given no specific guide-lines but was expected to mobilise private industry to co-operate with official agencies in working for the regeneration of the area.

This original Task Force was the forerunner of similar Task Forces and Inner City Action Teams in various parts of the country. They were supposed to work with, as well as galvanise, local authorities. Some local authorities understandably resented the loss of primacy in what they considered to be their own territory and sometimes the relationship between the two was prickly.

Aware that central government funding on any scale was out of the question, Michael Heseltine recommended the establishment of a Financial Institutions Group, comprising representatives from banks, building societies and pension funds. Their task was to advise the Department of the Environment on how to mobilise private investment for aiding the inner cities. On a visit to U.S.A. to learn from American experience on urban policy, the Group were impressed with their Urban Development Action Grant scheme as an instrument for attracting private funds and a scheme for Urban Development Grants was introduced in UK in 1982. These grants were payable for projects jointly funded by the public and private sectors to meet special needs in deprived areas.

Whether these moves were considered to be mere gestures or a genuine attempt to lay foundations for a better future, it was evident that not much benefit in terms of jobs could accrue from them until after the next election. This was confirmed beyond doubt when Mrs Thatcher decided to go to the polls a year earlier than her statutory obligation.

As unemployment had been rising continually throughout the whole country during her four years of office, there was never any possibility of a fall in the high unemployment Regions or cities. It is true that the percentage rise in some of the older stricken areas was less than in some of the places where unemployment was an unwelcome novelty. But statistical measures of magnitudes of misery are somewhat meaningless. More to the point was the human reality that many parts of the country were approximating to the condition against which the Roman Catholic Archbishop and Anglican Bishop of Liverpool forewarned several years earlier.

In a letter to the 'Times' in July 1980, they gave warning of the effects on local communities of high unemployment if the only cure proffered to their citizens of working age was to "get up and go". Such a policy they said: "... runs a grave risk of making inner cities and other priority areas of major cities into communities of the left behind. If our young people in any substantial numbers were to be successful in finding suitable employment elsewhere, the wound of this lost generation would leave a scar on the health of the community for decades to come."

CHAPTER FIVE
SOME FACTS AND FACETS OF THE LABOUR MARKET, 1945-1983

Manpower Policies in the Aftermath of War.

The schemes mentioned in the narrative for augmenting the labour force and expanding training opportunities in the early post-war years, affected only the fringe of the country's manpower. It was highly desirable to ensure that the great mass of workers untouched by such schemes were deployed in a way that was not wasteful or harmful to the national interest. Profiting from the lessons of 1914-18 Britain entered the conflict in 1939 without any illusions that she could get by on the voluntary system alone.

The National Service Acts and the Defence Regulations, especially 58a, which provided a legal basis for Essential Works Orders, gave the government virtually complete control of the labour force. Workers could be required to register and compelled to go to work that had been chosen for them and, over a large part of the industrial field, compelled to remain in jobs to which they had been sent.

Starting at the end of 1945 most of these controls were progressively removed and by 1st April 1947, the only industries in which controls still remained in force were coal-mining, building and agriculture. Workers were not allowed to leave these industries without permission of the Ministry of Labour and National Service.

The Economic Survey for 1947, published in February of that year, summarised the government's attitude to such controls in peacetime. In it they stated: "the government have now no direct control over the way in which manpower moves, although they can seek to influence the movement in a number of ways. The ideal distribution of manpower could not, in fact, be effected without complete powers of direction and would even then be limited by lack of accommodation." This renunciation of compulsion did not inhibit them in that same Survey from listing in tabular form a distribution of manpower by industry groups which it described as "neither an ideal distribution nor a forecast of what will happen but as the appropriate distribution needed to carry out the objectives proposed for 1947". They did not indicate how this "appropriate distribution" might be attained.

These brave words notwithstanding, the dislocation caused first by the fuel crisis then by the convertibility crisis of 1947, convinced the Government that the economy was not yet robust enough to operate without some controls over the movement of manpower.

Speaking in the House of Commons on 6 August 1947, Attlee stated: "We shall have to take some measure of control over the employment of labour. During the war we had to use full powers of direction of labour. It has been the desire of the government to move as quickly as possible towards restoration of freedom of the individual to undertake the kind of work he prefers. As things have turned out, it may be that we moved too far and too fast in this direction. We propose to reimpose the control over the engagement of labour that was almost universal during the war but has since been removed from all industries except coalmining, building and agriculture...It will be necessary to resume to a limited extent the use of powers of direction. This is not a resumption of the general powers of direction, but an essential supporting measure to enable the control of engagement to be effectively exercised."

A farcical side-show to the attempted controls on the movement of labour was the attempt, it might almost be said "by popular demand", to draw the "spivs" and "drones" into the work force. As the months after the war passed and people became more and more weary of the continuance of rationing and restrictions, some of their resentment boiled over onto that section of the populace which supposedly did well out of the black market (the "spivs") and those who managed to subsist without doing any work at all (the "drones").

146

In November 1947 the Government acted: the Registration for Employment Order (again under Regulation 58a) was issued, empowering the Minister of Labour to require the registration of persons with the same age limits as those subject to the Control of Engagement Order, who were either unoccupied or following certain occupations, e.g. betting, gambling (including pools and amusement arcades), night-clubs and street trading. There were to be two methods of registration: under one, individuals would have to register personally; under the other, employers were obliged to register their own employees. They would then be called for interview at an employment exchange and dealt with in exactly the same way as other persons seeking employment whilst subject to the Control of Engagement Order. In appropriate cases, they would be offered employment on essential work and, if necessary, directed to it.

When the exercise was completed in March the following year, nearly 71,000 men and women had been registered under the Order, about 1,700 had been placed in work of national importance and 17 (in a total labour force of around 20,400,000) directed to such work. Economically the exercise was a nonsense; politically, in view of the public mood, it showed good sense.

It was never intended that any of the controls over the movement of labour should be a permanent feature of the economy and on 1st January 1950, the ring fence around coalmining and agriculture was removed (the one round the building trade had been removed some months earlier). Early in March George Isaacs, the Minister of Labour and National Service, announced the ending of all other controls. In making the announcement, he commented that for a long period the government's powers to direct labour had in fact been in abeyance.

During the 2 1/2 years in which the Control of Engagement Order was in force only 29 compulsory direction orders were issued. (This figure excludes the 17 orders mentioned above, given to persons registering under the Registration for Employment Order.)

A curious sequel to Labour's restrictions on the movement of manpower was the introduction by the Conservative government in February 1952, a time of acute labour shortage in defence and export industries, of a most un-Conservative-like regulatory device, the Notification of Vacancies Order. This Order required employers to notify all their vacancies (apart from a few exempted categories) to an Employment Exchange. The main exemptions were for management and professional staff, vacancies for men and women of pensionable age, and, following wartime precedent, vacancies for boys and girls under eighteen.

Unlike the Control of Engagements Order, the new Order contained no provision for compelling workers to take jobs they did not want to. It was hoped that under this Order, Employment Exchange staff, aware of the full range of vacancies both in their own areas and farther afield and knowing which were the most important in the national interest, would be successful in persuading applicants to take these rather than the less important ones.

The Order remained in force until May 1956 when it was revoked, unmourned, unregretted and unresearched as to its value to the country (which was probably very little).

A Prime Minister Who Hated Unemployment.

Throughout his public life Harold Macmillan was deeply affected by the realisation of how much misery unemployment had brought to the lives of his constituents in Stockton-on-Tees for which he was first elected as Member of Parliament in 1924 at the age of 30. He describes the scene himself in his autobiography written some 30 years later. "I shall never forget," he wrote, "those despairing faces as the men tramped up and down the High Street in Stockton or gathered round the Five Lamps in Thornaby. Nor can any tribute be too great to the loyal, unflinching courage of the wives and mothers who somehow continued, often on a bare pittance, to provide for husbands and children and keep a decent home in being ...These grim conditions filled the background of my life and thoughts until the years immediately before the Second World War when rearmament and the substantial degree of recovery which followed the efforts of the National Government brought some alleviation."

An early indication of his views - regarded by most of his party colleagues as far too "socialistic" to be acceptable - was contained in a booklet Planning for Employment, signed by himself and 15 other MPs in 1932.

Better known to the general public was The Middle Way, published in 1938 in which his main concern was the poverty brought about by low wages as well as unemployment. Taking as his starting point the findings of Seebohm Rowntree (The Human Needs of Labour), and Sir John Boyd (Food, Health and Income), he set out to show how adequate nutrition for all could be provided.

When in 1963 unemployment rose to a new post-war peak, Macmillan let it be known how concerned he was about the situation. He particularly took issue with Professor Paish and those of like mind who were urging the government not to embark on a too expansionary course, commenting later, "against the old laissez-faire doctrine I reacted instinctively and violently".

Macmillan's views about unemployment did not change with the years. In a 1978 republication of The Middle Way, he wrote: "I have not changed the philosophy that underlines the work". In the Eighties, as Lord Stockton, he several times exhorted the Thatcher government to reflate in order to achieve higher output and more jobs.

This Tory grandee, who was a leading hawk in planning the Suez affair and who sacked a third of his Cabinet in one fell swoop in 1962, was no softie. But only a cynic would dismiss his concern about unemployment as a pose. Such views from a young Conservative MP in the Thirties were a barrier rather than a key to advancement and earned little but opprobrium from his fellow

Conservatives. In the 1980s, they listened to him with respect but without assent.

It is one of the ironies of history that the Prime Minister who had undoubtedly given more thought to the problem of unemployment than any of his predecessors or successors, never had to face a really serious unemployment situation in all of the six and three-quarter years of his premiership. There were recessions in 1958-59 and in 1962-63, but these were mere bubbles compared with the depression of the Thirties. In the first of these two recessions, unemployment never rose above 2.1% and in the second never above 2.4%. In January 1933 (though not on completely comparable figures) it was 23.0%.

S.E.T. The Stratagem that Never Quite Came Off.

Politicians of all parties were aware during the 1966 election campaign that whoever won the election would feel it necessary to introduce deflationary measures in order to reverse the deficit in the balance of payments and restore the strength of the pound. Potentially embarrassing to the government was the declaration by Callaghan (see p 47), shortly after the election date had been announced, that he did not foresee the need for severe increases in taxation.

The expression of such an opinion by so authoritative a source as the Chancellor of the Exchequer himself was to many members of the public as good as an undertaking not to raise taxes at all and certainly encouraged the government to search for some device which would raise revenue without too palpably increasing taxation. Nicholas (later Lord) Kaldor, Cambridge economist, who had been brought in as adviser to the government shortly after Labour's accession to power, produced a scheme which seemed just to fit the bill - Selective Employment Tax.

The only doubt which Members had on budget day was what forms the deflationary measures would take. They were, therefore, in Wilson's words, "dumbfounded", when, in his budget speech on 5

May, Callaghan, having told the House that it would be necessary to raise taxation to the tune of £250 million, then went on to say that there would be "no increase of income tax, surtax, purchase tax, vehicle licence duty or other Customs and Excise revenue duties".

After emphasising the major role in our exports played by manufacturing industry, Callaghan noted that between June 1960 and June 1965, employment in manufacturing industry rose by 142,000 but in services, distribution and construction by a million. "What is needed," he said, "is a differential tax which will increase the cost of labour in services and reduce the cost in manufacturing. I therefore propose to introduce a system to be called the Selective Employment Tax that will at one and the same time tax employment in services and construction but lessen the cost of employment in manufacturing."

This could be achieved by imposing on employers a tax of £1.25 per week per adult employee (rather less for women and young people). Manufacturing industry, but not the service industries or construction, would in due course receive a rebate. After explaining the method of collection Callaghan summarised his views on the merits of the tax as follows: "I believe that S.E.T. is a major step forward. It will prove in future years to be a very valuable addition to the measures available first as a means of raising revenue and also as an incentive for labour economies and manpower redeployment. The scheme will prove an easing on home demand this year, will open the way for a progressive strengthening of manufacturing industry and will make more resources available for exports with a beneficial effect on our balance of payments."

The tax was welcomed both by the Treasury who saw in it a good revenue raiser (£300 million in a full year) and by the DEA because they thought it would encourage higher productivity and help towards restructuring the economy. But Cabinet Ministers from other Departments, some of whom resented having it sprung on them with no time for discussion, were by no means all in favour of it. Crossman, in his Diaries, referred to it at different times as this "bloody tax", "absolutely unbearable" and as a "fatal mistake".

After initial surprise following the first announcement of the tax, it was condemned by most Conservatives as being too gimmicky and a harmful distortion of market forces. Moreover, as it would not begin to raise revenue until the following September, it had little relevance to the current economic situation. Iain Macleod, Shadow Chancellor, pledged the Conservatives to repeal it when they regained office. Nor did it go down well with the banking community at home or abroad, who felt that a government which was ready to acquiesce in a scheme which took so long to yield any revenue lacked zeal in its fight to restore the country's economic health.

Almost inevitably, it was unpopular with employers, especially those outside manufacturing, because of its effects on labour costs. It also got a hostile reception from many trade unionists and other Labour supporters, firstly because it was regarded as tantamount to a poll tax and, secondly, because it was likely to raise the price of everything bought and so increase the cost of living.

Bespattered by so much criticism, it is not surprising that it never achieved the permanency hoped for it by its authors. It was raised to £1.88 in the 1968 and £2.40 in the 1969 budget. The Conservatives reduced it to £1.20 in 1971 and with the introduction of Value Added Tax (VAT) in 1973, abolished it altogether.

Although a sturdy revenue-raiser, SET failed to achieve the redeployment of labour so much stressed by Callaghan on first presenting it. Even had his hopes been justified at the time two subsequent events were enough to stultify them. The first was the change in the economic climate from July 1966 onwards; the accent was now on deflation and lessening labour demands. Within a year of SET being introduced, unfilled vacancies had fallen from 439,000 to 262,000.

Secondly the government, in part abandonment of their original aims in introducing such a tax, shortly after devaluation abolished the rebate to employers in manufacturing industries, except in Development Areas. This action deprived the manufacturing sector of much of its former advantage over the service sector.

It proved quite impossible to assess the effect of SET on productivity. Professor Reddaway, who researched the matter in some depth, noted that there had been a big rise in productivity in distribution in the years immediately following its introduction, but was unable to say how far this was due to SET and how far to other factors, such as the abolition of retail price maintenance shortly before the end of the previous Conservative government.

Perhaps the last word should be left to Callaghan himself. Writing in his Memoirs, 'Time and Chance', about the major tax reforms he introduced, he stated; "The only unsuccessful new venture was the Selective Employment Tax".

The Metamorphoses of the Employment Service.

The establishment of a national system of labour exchanges (renamed employment exchanges in 1916) was largely the result of the vigorous advocacy of Winston Churchill, President of the Board of Trade at that time. Having persuaded the Cabinet that they were a vital complement to the unemployment insurance scheme which the Liberal government were about to inaugurate, he piloted the Labour Exchanges Bill through the House of Commons in May 1909. The first exchanges were opened on 1 February 1910 and Churchill (never exactly a laggard in any enterprise he was promoting) visited, according to his son-biographer, all seventeen exchanges in the London area on opening day.

He was at pains to stress the positive role which he hoped these exchanges would play in the labour market, declaring, "they are primarily agents for dealing with employment rather than unemployment"; by informing those seeking work where to go and where not to go, they would "diminish local and accidental unemployment".

The exchanges hardly had time to prove their worth before the first World War broke out and they found themselves deeply involved in recruiting for the forces and essential industries.

In the years of high unemployment between the wars, they were swamped, especially in the slump years, by unemployed workers signing on for their dole and enquiring, usually with little hope, what jobs, if any, were available. In 1939, and for some six years afterwards, their main task was once again to recruit in war time for the forces and for essential industry. For several decades after the second world war the employment exchanges were as much extended in trying to relieve the labour shortages of employers as in trying to find jobs for the unemployed.

In the 1960s, the belief gained ground that the public employment services could make an important contribution to economic growth ("growth" having become the lodestar of economic policy in virtually all countries).

In 1970, this belief was articulated in two documents, a consultative document on The Future of the Employment Service, issued by the Department of Employment and Productivity, and a Report on Manpower Policy in the United Kingdom, published by OECD. The Labour government was out of office by the time consultations on the DEP document were completed and it was left to Heath's Conservative government to follow up the result of these consultations and also to decide what heed, if any, should be taken of the carefully-worded but critical comments of the OECD on the British employment services.

Two documents and three years later, the Conservatives' plans took shape when the Employment and Training Act 1973, was passed.

This Act provided for a new body to be set up, the Manpower Services Commission (MSC).

The MSC was to have a full-time chairman and nine part-time members nominated by the TUC (3), CBI (3), local authorities (2), plus one professional educationist. It would have two executive arms: the Training Services Agency (TSA) and the Employment Services Agency (ESA). It would be directly funded by the government, although the Secretary of State for Employment would be responsible to Parliament for its efficient operation and the proper use of its funds.

One of the early tasks of the MSC was to extend nationwide the system of Job Centres already operating in some parts of the country. These were to be located in main streets rather than in dingy back streets where so many of the employment exchanges had been located in the past. Users of this new service would find themselves in rooms where the decor was brighter and the layout more functionally designed than in the old-fashioned employment exchanges. Nor would they be seeking work or advice cheek-by-jowl with a shuffling dole queue. Unemployment offices were to be separately housed and the system of paying benefit by post, already started experimentally, was to be gradually extended to the whole country.

The object of these innovations was threefold. The first was to make the service the first, not the last resort of both employers looking for workers and workers seeking employment. This could best be done by supplying customers with the maximum information about what was on offer. Gone was the obscurantist practice of keeping job information under the counter. Details of job vacancies and training opportunities were now posted on display boards for all to see.

The second object was to attract a less down-at-heel type of client. The old exchanges had always been better informed about manual than white collar jobs and more utilised by manual than white collar workers. But in the outside world, the ratio of manual to white collar jobs was steadily diminishing. Unless the new Job Centres could attract more of this trade they would lose much of their relevance.

The third object was to improve manpower intelligence. The market philosophy had not yet come into its own and in the early Seventies, both Labour and Conservative governments set considerable store by manpower planning. Regional Planning Councils and Regional Planning Boards were called on to provide manpower plans both for their own use - so that they did not run into unnecessary labour shortages - and for the government's use so that they could ensure that money spent on training and educational facilities was not misdirected.

The Job Centres, like the Unemployment Benefit Offices, were expected to provide for the government not only statutory and goodwill statistics, but also information about the mood and moves of employers in their areas.

The 1973 Employment and Training Act, which set up the ESA and the TSA, also made provision for the reorganisation of the Youth Employment Service. This service had originally been set up under the Employment and Training Act 1948, and over most of the country had been run by the local education authorities reporting to the Regional Representative of the Ministry of Labour/Department of Employment. However, in parts of Scotland and in most of South West England, it was run directly by Ministry of Labour/Department of Employment staff. This arrangement was workable but administratively untidy and illogical. The 1973 Act made it mandatory on local authorities to provide an advisory and placement service for "persons who are attending either full-time or part-time, educational institutions in Great Britain other than universities".

The title "Youth Employment Service" was dropped in favour of "Careers Service" and the new Service was inaugurated on 1 April 1974, the same date as the new county structure in England and Wales came into being. Each county was now responsible for running its own Careers Service and lubricating the whole system was the insistence that all engaged in the Careers Service should receive longer and better training than in the past.

The aim of the new-look service both for young people and adults was a service which would be held in high esteem by employers and workers and increasingly used by both. A survey carried out by the MSC in 1978 when 418 Job Centres were in operation, showed that they were placing 50% more people into employment than the employment exchanges they had replaced, the increase in placings being especially notable in non-manual occupations. Especially popular amongst job seekers was the self-service system of displaying vacancies which users of the service found quick, convenient and efficient.

Most of the DE staff had argued for many years that their placing and advisory service should be housed separately from the unemployment benefit offices and given more attractive premises; only thus, they claimed, could they free themselves from the dole image which was such a deterrent to its usage by reputable employers and high calibre workers. These figures seemed to justify that claim.

But not everyone was so pleased with this development. Professor Layard put forward the view that by distancing itself from the unemployed, the new employment service was aggravating the very problem it was there to solve. This view was reinforced by an examination of employers' attitudes to the public employment service carried out by the Department of Social Sciences, Loughborough University of Technology; the conclusion reached was that the new service was detrimental to the interests of the long-term unemployed. The main reason they cited for this conclusion was as follows.

Employers expected Job Centre staff to do some preliminary screening of applicants before submitting them to a vacancy. However, these employers, as has been pointed out elsewhere, regarded with suspicion anyone who had been 'on the dole' for any length of time.

Employment service staff were therefore chary about submitting such applicants if there were suitable candidates who had only recently come on to their books.

The social scientists summed up their findings in these words: "While measures such as 'placement penetration' and 'market share' of vacancies are highlighted as means of judging the success of Job Centres, the emphasis is likely to be on meeting employer requirements via screening, to the detriment of the long-term unemployed."

In the late Sixties, when Barbara Castle was initiating reforms to the public employment service, unemployment stood at little over half a million and it could well be argued that what the country most needed was an agency which would help to deploy the workforce to a pattern more conducive to economic growth. The unemployed would benefit incidentally rather than as the main recipient of employment service attention.

By the time Professor Layard was writing and the social scientists from Loughborough were reporting, unemployment was shooting up rapidly. Willy-nilly the public employment service was once again fully occupied trying to help the unemployed directly. The first aim of Job Centre staff was to guide their clients to suitable jobs or training; if this failed, their next option was to get them on to one of the Special Employment Schemes by which the government hoped to take the sting out of unemployment as a political issue without jeopardising their now successful anti-inflation policy. Plus ça change, plus c'est la même chose.

The Training that Wasn't.

We have already mentioned (see p 13) how immediately after the war the government increased the number of Government Training Centres (GTCs) from 17 in 1945 to 65 in 1946. In doing this, they had two aims in view: the first was to help ex-Servicemen and women to acquire the sort of skills which would enable them to find jobs; the second was to make a small (it could never be more than that) contribution to easing industry's labour shortages.

This momentum very soon came to an end and by the time Labour ceded office to the Conservatives in 1951, only 22 GTCs remained in operation. Training, it was almost universally conceded, was the job of industry. Industry agreed with that viewpoint but, unfortunately, with a few honourable exceptions, did very little about it.

By the mid-Fifties, Britain's industrial lead over her main competitors was ebbing away as the rest of Europe recovered from the ravages of war. It became evident that one reason why they were doing so much better than Britain in terms of economic growth was the attention they paid to training their labour forces. Other countries also benefited from the comparative absence of restrictive practices which were such a clogging influence over British industry.

The quantity and quality of training in industry had relevance not only to the level of output but also to the career prospects of young people about to start their working lives. An opportunity for industry to improve its training standards and for more youngsters to find satisfying careers would present itself from the mid Fifties onwards, when the number of young people reaching school leaving age would rise from about 647,000 in 1957 to 929,000 in 1962.

With this in mind, the Ministry of Labour's National Joint Advisory Committee appointed a Sub-Committee under the chairmanship of its Parliamentary Secretary Robert Carr to consider the matter. The terms of reference given to the Sub-Committee were: "To consider the arrangements for training young workers in industry, in particular reference to the adequacy of intake into apprenticeship and other forms of training in the light of the expected increase in the number of young persons entering employment and the need to ensure an adequate supply of young workers for future needs."

The Commission reported in early 1958; it stressed that the existing intake to industry was inadequate and that this bulge of school leavers presented a unique opportunity to put things right. It was not the function of government to provide this training; it should limit itself to doing those things which industrial employers found it difficult to do, such as organising group training schemes and gearing up technical colleges and other institutions of further education to deal with the off-the-job aspect of training. It scarcely dipped its toes into the dangerous waters of length of training, age of entry restrictions and other impediments to creating a training scheme which could bear comparison with those in Germany, Sweden and other leading industrial countries.

The three main results of the Carr Report were: first, the establishment of a Central Training Council (albeit toothless) to promote more and better training on a national scale; second, the expansion of GTCs to provide "model" examples of training methods; and third, the promotion of group training schemes whereby small firms collectively could provide more thorough training than was possible on their own.

Unfortunately, the Report was published at a time when the economy was entering its worst recession since the war (unemployment in 1958 averaged just over 2% for the first time since the 1946 Act came into operation). The shortage of labour was temporarily abated and, training being a peripheral activity with all too many firms, the Report never gave the spurt to training which its authors and sponsors had hoped.

With the upturn of the economy in 1959, it became more obvious than ever that Britain was lagging behind in industrial training and the re-elected Conservative government gave the matter further consideration. Wedded though they were to the principle of voluntarism, it was so obvious that voluntarism had failed that they now introduced a scheme which would compel firms to give their employees appropriate training or suffer financially if they failed to do so.

The scheme would operate as follows: a bill would be passed empowering the Ministry of Labour to set up tripartite Training Boards to cover defined sections of industry. They would function by imposing a levy on all except the smallest firms, but this levy would be recoverable by firms which reached approved standards of training.

To many people these proposals constituted the most hopeful development in the training world since the war; it not only introduced an element of compulsion without which it was clear that Britain's training standards would continue to languish, but they were also - though less so later - untarnished by the unhelpful party bickering which so often hampers or negates innovatory undertakings. The Industrial Training Bill, though framed by a Conservative government, was passed virtually without alteration by the newly elected Labour government in 1964.

The process of appointing representatives to each Board from employers, trade unions and other interests, was inevitably a slow one, but eventually 23 Boards were constituted covering over 50% of the country's workforce. One of the most important in size, influence and originality was the Engineering Industry Training Board. They introduced the module system of training which was more flexible and more comprehensive than the time-serving system of apprenticeship, so beloved by trade union traditionalists.

There is no doubt that, taking the whole range of training, positive progress was made in its quantity and quality as a result of the 1964 Act. But other countries too were making progress in those years and it is doubtful whether in this difficult-to-measure field there was any closing of the gap between Britain and her competitors. Moreover, although the 1964 Act was in all essentials Conservative-drafted, when the party regained office in 1970, many MPs came back to Westminster their ears ringing with complaints from (mainly small) employers to whom the very idea of a levy-rebate scheme was abhorrent.

Once again Britain's training arrangements came under review and in 1972, the government issued a Consultative Paper on "Training and the Future". Under the 1973 Employment and Training Act which followed, provision was made for the levy-grant system to be converted to a levy-exemption scheme under which ITBs were no longer required to raise a levy and were prohibited from raising above 1% of their payrolls. There was particular concern at that time about the disproportionate number of young people who were unemployed and, in May 1977, Geoffrey Holland, Head of Planning in the MSC, issued a Report, "Young People and Work", in which he emphasised that unemployment amongst young people was now a structural feature of the economy and would not disappear once trade picked up.

The government's response was the Youth Opportunities Programme to start in September 1978; this scheme offered six months work experience to unemployed young people in the 16-18 age group. Training provided in these Programmes was minimal and although in the early days of the scheme over 80% of those participating found jobs within seven months, by 1981 unemployment having risen by more than a million since the scheme's inception, this figure had fallen to 40%.

With the advent of a Conservative government in 1979, the picture changed in two ways: first, the country now had a government which was more anti-interventionist than any of its post-war predecessors; secondly, unemployment was rising at a pace only equalled in the early days of the 1930s slump. Both factors helped to shape government policy towards industrial training.

The new policy was well exemplified by the way they disposed of the Industrial Training Boards. To those who shared the Thatcherite beliefs they represented all that was abominable - interventionism, corporatism, and financial impositions on wealth creating industry. Following a review by the MSC the government announced in November 1981 that 15 of the 23 ITBs were to be abolished, despite recommendations by the MSC to the contrary.

More newsworthy and directly affecting more people, was the New Training Initiative announced by Norman Tebbit towards the end of 1981. The main feature of this New Training Initiative was the introduction of a Youth Training Scheme (YTS) under which, starting in September 1983, all young people under the age of 18 would have the opportunity of either continuing in full-time education or of entering a period of planned work experience combined with work-related training and education. The cost in a full year would be around £1 billion compared with a cost of £400 million in the same period for the Youth Opportunities Programme which YTS would replace.

It might seem strange that a government supposedly dedicated to laissez-faire principles should be prepared to spend so much on a function which it had always proclaimed to be the duty of industry. The explanation is two-fold. To train the country's youth (or indeed the labour force of any age) helps to improve the supply side of the labour market, a matter in which the government had always acknowledged its responsibility. Secondly, although public opinion was quiescent about unemployment in general there was widespread concern about the social consequences of having thousands of young people roaming about with nothing to do - the riots and burnings of 1980 and 1981 were still fresh in people's minds. Though the ideal of full employment might be a fantasy of the past, the voting implications of seeming indifferent to unemployment of the young would be very much a reality of the next election if nothing were done about it.

By the time of this election, the first signs of economic recovery were visible, although it was too early for this to be reflected in the always laggard unemployment figures. What was apparent was that in the now weakening recession, recidivist Britain had followed its traditional malpractice of cutting back on training, thereby guaranteeing multiple skill shortages once recovery gathered momentum.

Special Employment Measures.

By the mid-Seventies, Labour were presiding over a post-war peak of unemployment. This placed them on the horns of a very difficult dilemma. If they reflated to any significant extent, they would wreck their anti-inflation policy; if they deflated, there was no possibility of bringing unemployment down to anything like its post-war norm. Whereas right up to the time of the Barber boom getting unemployment down was regarded as the first political imperative, by the mid-Seventies, as has been noted, the top priority was to get inflation down.

What the government did was to introduce a number of Special Employment Measures which would be targeted directly at the unemployed, thereby avoiding the inflationary effect of a more generalised expansion. Though introduced by the 1974-79 Labour government, they were continued and extended by the following Conservative government who were operating in a far worse employment situation. By April 1982, the numbers employed on these schemes were as shown below:

Table 17

Youth Opportunities Programme (YOP)	190,000
Temporary Short-Time Working Compensation Scheme (TSTWCS)	113,000
Job Release Scheme (JRS)	67,000
Young Workers Scheme (YWS)	51,000
Special Temporary Employment Scheme (STEP)	28,000
Community Enterprise Programme (CEP)	7,000
TOTAL	456,000

Source: Department of Employment Gazette

Youth Opportunities Programme was an omnibus term comprising several types of employment and training. Priority on these courses was given to school leavers and other 16 to 17 year olds who had been unemployed for three months. Young persons outside these age limits were also admitted to them if places were available. The courses fell into one of two categories, work experience and work preparation.

Three types of work experience were on offer. Work Experience on Employers Premises (WEEP) placed young people directly with employers in a wide range of industry. Community Projects (CP) provided services of value to the community, for example, environmental improvement schemes, whilst Training Workshops (TW) offered training in basic skills.

Work preparation courses were usually held at educational establishments and skill centres, although many of them included short placements with an employer. There were two main types of course, both lasting 13 weeks. Short Training Courses (STCs) aimed to equip young people for work at semi-skilled or operator level and Work Introduction Courses (WTCs) aimed to help low achievers to acquire basic work, communication and numeracy skills.

The Temporary Short-Time Working Compensation Scheme (TSTWCS) was the direct descendant of two earlier schemes: the Temporary Employment Subsidy (TES) and the Short-Time Working Compensation Scheme (STWC).

TES, first introduced in August 1975, provided that employers prepared to defer an impending redundancy affecting more than ten workers in an establishment could qualify for a subsidy of £20 per week for each full-time job maintained. After one year, subject to checks by DE staff, a supplement of £10 was payable for a maximum of six months to employees still faced with redundancies.

Employers representing nearly all industries took advantage of the scheme at some time or other, but the largest beneficiaries were the textile, clothing and footwear industries. This caused the EEC Commission to complain that these industries were gaining an unfair advantage over their competitors and in May 1978, a modified scheme was introduced, the Short-Time Working Compensation Scheme (STWCS) under which the government paid 75% of the wages of employees put on short-time. Applications for both TES and STWCS ceased to be accepted after 31 March 1979.

On 1 April 1979, the Temporary Short-Time Working Scheme was introduced. Like the two previous schemes, it was aimed at avoiding redundancies, but with the promise that employees put on short-time must return to the firms for a normal day's work after a maximum of seven consecutive idle days. Up to 30 June 1979, employees could qualify for this compensation for short-time working for a maximum period of twelve months; from 1 July the maximum period was reduced to six months. Engineering, especially mechanical engineering, was the largest user of this facility.

The Job Release Scheme (JRS), introduced in January 1977, offered workers within a year of retirement an allowance if they would withdraw from the employment field, thereby creating a vacancy for younger workers. The initiative for applying for this facility rested with the individual and his application would only go forward with the agreement of his employer. At first the scheme was operative only in assisted areas, but from 1 April 1978, it was extended to cover the whole country and, in May 1979, men became eligible for the scheme at the age of 62, the age of eligibility for women remaining at 59.

As has been mentioned earlier, although public opinion was little stirred by the rise in unemployment amongst adults in the late

Seventies and early Eighties, there was widespread concern about the huge number of jobless young people. It was believed by many people and often averred by the 1979 Conservative government that one reason for such high unemployment amongst the young was that trade union pressure was maintaining juvenile wages well above the market clearing rate.

To help obviate this impediment the government introduced in January 1982 its Young Workers Scheme. This scheme entitled employers to claim £15 a week for each employee under 18 whose earnings were less than £50 per week.

The Special Temporary Employment Scheme (STEP), introduced in June 1977, was a successor to the Job Creation Programme (JCP) started nearly two years earlier. The object of JCP was to provide temporary jobs of social value for people who would otherwise be unemployed. The people for whom it catered were those between 16 and 24 and the over-fifties. In due course the young element came under the aegis of the Youth Opportunities Programme and provision for adults was made under STEP, soon to be renamed the Community Enterprise Scheme (CES) in 1981. The clients of CES were those aged 19 to 24 who had been unemployed for over six months and those aged 25 and over who had been continuously unemployed for over a year.

The sort of projects undertaken by STEP teams were tree planting, clearing derelict land, helping pensioners, insulating houses and cataloguing archives. Local authorities (60%) and voluntary organisations (30%) were the main sponsors. Men and women working in these schemes were paid the rate for the job and sponsors were allowed to draw on public funds to cover administrative costs.

Supply Side Economics and the Labour Market.

Between the early Seventies and the mid-Eighties the world changed from one in which maintaining and, if necessary, boosting demand was held to be the key to economic health to one in which the key role was assigned to constraining demand. In 1971, when ultra-Keynesian expansion was the order of the day and the United Kingdom was experiencing the Barber boom, President Nixon was proclaiming, "I am a Keynesian now." Ten years later, President Reagan was preaching the virtues of tackling the economic problems of the day by improving the supply side of the labour market. Margaret Thatcher in the UK had already been treading that path for some eighteen months.

Keynes, once the non-pareil amongst economists, was now blamed as a major contributor to the world-wide inflation which was held to be largely the result of over-stimulating demand in the pursuit of full employment. The counterpart of this over-stimulation of the demand side of the labour market was neglect of the important supply side.

The charge against Keynes that in his General Theory he downgraded the supply side certainly has some substance in it. In the second paragraph of his eighteenth chapter, 'The General Theory of Employment Re-Stated', he declares "We take as given the existing skill and quantity of available equipment, the existing technique, the degree of competition, the tastes and habits of the consumer, the disutility of different intensities of labour and of the activities of supervision and organisation as well as the social structure...This does not mean that we assume these factors to be constant; but merely that, in this place and context, we are not considering or taking into account the effects and consequences of changes in the world."

This is a mighty lot to side-line and in doing so, we emerge into a world no longer anchored to reality.

In defence of Keynes, it should be remembered that the General Theory, published in 1936, was written at a time when the whole industrialised world was suffering from and baffled by the sharp fall in demand. It seemed logical to believe that the way to prevent further slumps was to stimulate demand when it seemed to be flagging.

The further charge that Keynes was ignorant of or indifferent to the economic and human consequences of inflation has no substance. To see that this is so one only has to read The Economic Consequences of the Peace (1919), or How to Pay for the War (1940).

Both Reagan and Thatcher saw the situation they were confronted with as one of excess rather than deficient demand. What induced them to concentrate their efforts on the supply side of the labour market was not so much the musings of theoretical economists as the manifest failure of demand management either to create jobs in the long term or restrain inflation.

Supply side champions set great store by the disincentive effects of high taxation, especially direct taxation. Any Chancellor, therefore, it was held, who reduced taxation was doing right by his country; patriotism would walk hand in hand with popularity.

The Thatcher government made a start in this direction when Geoffrey Howe, in his first budget, knocked 3p off the standard rate of income tax and reduced the higher rate from 83p to 60p in the pound. The Reagan government soon followed suit by cuts in the Federal income tax of 5% in 1981, 10% in 1982 and 10% in 1983.

Another aim which Reagan and Thatcher held in common was a determination to reduce the amount of money going out on social security. In both countries, regulations were tightened up and eligibility conditions made more strict. These economies, it was claimed, would benefit the economy in two ways. The income tax cuts would provide an incentive for entrepreneurs and managers to operate more efficiently and more adventurously, whilst those at the poverty end of society would be encouraged to help themselves rather than rely on the state to provide.

A major target for Mrs Thatcher was the trade unions. They, it was held, harmed the economy in two ways. By imposing restrictive practices on industry they impaired its efficiency and by raising wages above the market clearing rate they created unemployment. There was too the political angle; trade unions had bedevilled the 1964-70 Labour government, brought down the 70-74 Conservative government and infuriated the country by their Winter of Discontent in 1979. Moreover, their inclusion on various Quangos and consultative bodies entailed exactly the corporative approach to politics which Mrs Thatcher treated with such disdain.

However, as with the miners, Mrs Thatcher did not rush her fences, restrained perhaps to some extent by the presence at the Department of Employment of the more consensus-minded Jim Prior. Nevertheless, by the time of the 1983 election, legislation had been passed prohibiting secondary picketing, enjoining secret ballots before strike action was taken and severely limiting the scope and legality of closed shops.

Trade unions were not regarded as the only organisations hampering the free working of the labour market. Wages Councils, introduced by the then Liberal Winston Churchill in 1909 as Trade Boards, were not spared by their lineage or longevity and were drastically reduced in number. By keeping wages artificially high, it was argued, they generated unemployment. Still less was there room in a free economy for such interventionist bodies as the Prices Commission abolished in 1980 and the National Enterprise Board abolished in 1981.

Another *sine qua non* of achievement in the supply side of the labour market is improvement in the quality and quantity of training. A summary of the successes and more notable failures in this field was given earlier this chapter.

The Employment and Unemployment of Women.

Since 1945 there has been a huge increase in the variety of jobs done by women and in the number of women who have taken up work outside the home. Working outside the home is not a new phenomenon in the history of women. In the early days of the industrial revolution many working-class women were faced with the choice of accepting work in mines or factories or of seeing their families starve. The Victorian middle-class conscience (or the conscience of a section of the Victorian middle-class) recoiled at such exploitation and a succession of Acts was passed to limit the hours and regulate the conditions of work for both women and children.

Employment in factory or mine was not the only work which women undertook outside the home. Millions of them worked as domestic servants in the homes of the well-to-do.

When the First World War broke out, women undertook a variety of work which they had not undertaken before - in munitions, engineering, transport, agriculture and the welfare services. The male-dominated trade unions soon levered them out of these jobs once the war was over.

Women played an even more crucial role in the second world war not only in industry and other facets of civilian life but also as enrolled members of the army, navy and airforce.

Curiously insensitive to women's aspirations and capabilities was that staunch advocate of pre-1914 Liberal measures and saviour of his country in war-time, Winston Churchill. Implacably opposed to the suffragettes before the First World War, he found time in the last weeks of the caretaker government to comment when writing of demobilisation plans: "Women are an entirely different category [from men!]. They do not mutiny or cause disturbances, and the sooner they are back in their homes the better."

As after the 1914-18 war, so after that of 1939-45 there was a big trek of women back to their homes. It seemed as though history was about to repeat itself, which is exactly what it was not going to do. In terms of international indebtedness, Britain was nearer bankruptcy in 1945 than in 1918. She could not maintain essential services, expand exports and initiate the social reforms to which the government were committed, with an overwhelmingly male labour force. As mentioned earlier (see p 12), a special campaign was launched in 1947 to attract women back to work. From that time onwards, both the proportion of females in the labour force and the variety of jobs which they filled, have continued to expand.

A few statistics will give a good idea of the trend. In 1948, females constituted 33.5% of the labour force; by 1960, this had risen to 35.5%, by 1970 to 37.7% and by 1980 to 41.1%. In 1951, 25% of women were in paid employment, by 1971 the proportion had risen to 41% and by 1981 to 55.5. The number of women in the labour force rose from 7.8 million in 1959 to 10.3 million in 1979; during the same period, the number of men in the labour force fell from 16.4 million to 16.1 million.

Four factors have combined to bring about this change in the gender composition of the labour force. First is the increasing availability of labour-saving devices and of fast and take-away foods. The running of a home, except where there are children or dependent relatives, is no longer a full-time job.

Second has been the growth of non-manual compared with manual jobs. Whilst manufacturing jobs of all kinds have been declining, those in the service industries have been expanding. The latter have not only generated more jobs in activities traditionally performed by women, such as catering, cleaning, hairdressing, hospitals; but have also opened new vistas in financial services, especially banking and building societies.

Third has been the huge rise in part-time employment. Both demand and supply factors have brought this about. Employers in many areas have found that they could not recruit the workers they wanted unless they showed flexibility in hours whilst many women who would have ruled out full-time work have found that with a little bit of organisation (and help at home from their husbands) they could manage a part-time job.

Fourth and intermingled with all the others, has been the changing attitudes of both men and women towards women taking up work outside the home. That is not to say that even now they enjoy equality in status and conditions when they are employed. The Equal Pay Act of 1970, with its later amendments and the Sex Discrimination Act of 1975, have flattened some of the bulwarks but not seriously imperilled the citadel of male dominance in office and factory. For many years, whilst most professions yielded at least theoretical equality to women, both the Temples of God and the Temples of Mammon held out, unyielding either to the assaults of feminism or the blandishments of reason. Not until the late Sixties did the latter agree to admit women as stockbrokers, whilst women were debarred from the priesthood in U.K. until as late as 1994.

Whether progress towards sex equality in employment is swift, slow or halts altogether, the changing role of women at work and at home is altering the pattern of employment. Up to 1977, women could opt out of paying full insurance if they were insured through their husbands. This meant that they were not entitled to any benefit if they became unemployed. Consequently, many of the unemployed women felt that it was not worthwhile registering for work and so did not appear in the official statistics of unemployment. Now that this option is no longer open to them, these figures should become more accurate in this respect than in the past. Even so, the tug between home and outside work is likely to remain stronger with women than with men and women's "activity rates" (i.e. the proportion of women of working age who engage in paid employment) are likely to remain somewhat below those for men. The typical figure of the 1930s was the male breadwinner with one or more children. Many women, as so often happens in hard times, made enormous sacrifices for their families. (Harold Macmillan, as mentioned earlier, in his book, The Middle Way, referred to "the loyal, unflinching courage of the wives and mothers.") Such sacrifices by so many on such a scale should not be necessary in the future, although no doubt this picture will still be true of a number of families. Nor must the plight of one-parent families, male as well as female, be forgotten. These constitute one of the major poverty groups in the country and very often they have to cope with debilitating psychological and emotional problems.

What has been lacking has been any decisive inroads by women into the more senior and prestigious jobs in industry and the professions. Nor has there been adequate provision of nursery or creche facilities to enable young mothers to go out to work.

Some Important Voices in the Unemployment Debate.

It is obviously impossible to expound and evaluate within the confines of a small sub-chapter of a medium-sized book the ideas of the principal economists who have influenced thought on the matter of unemployment. All that is attempted here is to summarise very briefly the content and significance of their thinking on this particular aspect of economics. I do so, however, very conscious of the omissions.

Karl Marx, 1818-1883.

To Marx, unemployment was an essential feature of the transition from capitalism to socialism. Marx accepted the contention of David Ricardo (1772-1823) that the value of a commodity was to be measured by the amount of labour involved in its production. If, therefore, a worker produced ten units of production in a day and was paid the equivalent of six, then the value of the remaining four would be surplus. And where did this surplus go? To the capitalist employer, of course. Bully, one might think, for the capitalist. Not so; he (or his descendants) would in due course get their own come-uppance.

How was all this to come about? It all starts, according to Marx, with the mode of production, which determines the nature of each historical epoch. Class antagonism and class struggles are the force behind the change from one mode of production to another. Thus, just as the landlords of the feudal system had to yield power to the bourgeoisie as a result of the new practices in agriculture and industry, so the bourgeoisie would eventually have to yield power to the proletariat.

Profit being the driving force of capitalism, each employer is competing with his fellows. In order to do so successfully he must keep his costs down to a minimum. This he will do by the accumulation of more and more capital so that he can invest in the most up-to-date plant. Employers utilise two types of capital, constant capital consisting of raw materials, tools and machinery, and variable capital consisting of human labour. When output rises employers increase their demand for labour and wages rise. But the benefit to wage earners is short-lived. Employers soon introduce more machinery and part of the labour force is discharged. The victims of this process constitute "the reserve army of unemployed". This reserve army forms an integral part of the structure of capitalism.

The relentless competition which impels employers to hire and fire this marginal labour force as it suits them will, according to Marx, be the downfall of capitalism. "Capitalism," he states in *Das Kapital* "begets with the inexorability of a law of nature its own negation."

As the worker becomes more and more the slave of the machine he becomes more and more alienated from the system in which he is a helpless cog. Adding to the "immiseration" of the workers is the growing "industrial reserve army" of the unemployed. These unemployed will combine in the end with the low-paid workers to revolt against their bourgeois bosses. The expropriators will be expropriated and there will be no more exploitation of the worker or the sentencing of would-be workers to idleness they never sought.

This is how it should have worked out, but of course it has not. It would be wrong, however, for the capitalist to be too exultant over the failures of incompetent and often cruel and repressive Marxist regimes. The capitalist system has over the years achieved a far higher standard of living for its citizens than has communism, but the way the wealth it creates is distributed leaves a lot to be desired. Moreover, modern capitalism, particularly in its new multi-national mode of production, still thrives on the existence, especially in Third World countries, of an "industrial reserve army" of unemployed.

John Maynard (later Lord) Keynes (1883-1946).

For some twenty years after the war, Keynes was accorded a veneration seldom if ever before accorded to an exponent of the "dismal science". The golden key (or so it seemed at the time) which he proffered to the world, was his concept of "aggregate demand".

The classical economists, according to Keynes, had lived in a world of illusion. Where they had gone wrong was in their acceptance of Says Law. This law was propounded by the French economist, Jean Baptiste Say (1767-1832) and taught that since production, by wages or profits, created a similar demand, an economy was always tending towards an equilibrium in which all resources of capital and labour would be fully employed.

Keynes pointed out that this was patently untrue of the world of the Thirties or, if it was happening, full employment would only be achieved in the long run and, as he has so often been quoted as saying, in the long run we are all dead. Keynes' refutation of these orthodox economists was contained in The General Theory of Employment Interest and Money, published in 1936. The level of employment, he pointed out, depends on the aggregate demand created by investment and consumption expenditure. If in combination they failed to employ the available labour then the result is involuntary unemployment.

But there were several things which a government could do to augment demand for labour. They could unbalance the budget; they could reduce taxes; they could encourage investment by lowering interest rates and they could create jobs directly by public works and by improving what in later years became known as the infra-structure.

The Achilles heel of the Keynesian system was the impetus it gave to inflation, a phenomenon to which Keynes paid little attention in the The General Theory. This was not because he failed to realise the human and economic damage it could do, but because at the time he was writing, the industrial world was still suffering from the calamitous effects of the world-wide fall in prices which had started in U.S.A. and spread throughout the globe.

By the mid-Seventies, some economists and politicians felt that the inflationary propensities of the Keynesian physic more than outweighed any benefits it might confer in terms of employment. Sir Keith Joseph, in his 1974 Preston speech (see p 93), and James Callaghan in his address to the Labour party in 1976 (see p 105), might be said to have delivered their respective epitaphs on Keynesianism.

Others believed that these obsequies were premature. James Meade and the "neo-Keynesians" believed that though Keynesian-type demand management as applied in practice might be flawed, it could still succeed if accompanied by a workable incomes policy. Both new and old Keynesians were dismissed by the monetarists as being wrong-headed and irrelevant.

At the end of the war there was general agreement in UK that it was essential for social harmony and fair dealing to prevent the unemployment which caused so much suffering in the years before.

This successive governments succeeded in doing for over twenty years, but as time went on, it became more and more difficult to maintain the requisite level of demand without engendering an unacceptable level of inflation. Everyone (except the minority who profit nicely from it) was fed up with this inflation and in 1979, elected a government which was determined to conquer inflation no matter what the cost. This they virtually succeeded in doing for a time but only by dint of inflicting on several million of their citizens the misery and indignity of unemployment.

In fact he did no such thing. Although, very fairly, he proposed that unemployment benefit should be payable indefinitely so long as the recipient was genuinely unemployed, he made recommendations designed to prevent avoidable idleness which, if less crude, were in many respects more stringent than those brought into effect by the Thatcher government, viz

(i)

"Men and women in receipt of unemployment benefit cannot be allowed to hold out indefinitely for work of the type to which they are used to or in their present places of residence, if there is work which they could do available at the standard wage for that work."

(ii)

"Men and women who have been unemployed for a certain period should be required as a condition of continued benefit to attend a work or training centre, such attendance being designed as a means of preventing habituation to idleness and as a means of improving their capacity for earning. Incidentally, though this is an altogether minor reason for the proposal, such a condition is the most effective way of unmasking the relatively few persons who may be suspected of malingering, who have perhaps some concealed means of earning which they are combining with an appearance of unemployment."

When Beveridge was writing his Report the country was in the middle of a war which caused immeasurable suffering in this country and throughout the world. The prevailing mood in Britain was not to get back to the pre-war world but to a better one, in particular, to get rid of the mass unemployment which was at the root of so many of the evils of that world. Doing so proved easier for a decade or two more than anyone thought possible. Then it all collapsed. If the conviction, so widely held in those days, that mass unemployment is a moral outrage, had survived into the seventies and eighties, then perhaps the country would not have accepted its return with such supine fatalism.

Milton Friedman (1912 -)
In contrast to Keynes, whose aim was to show how beneficial government intervention could be if rightly timed, Milton Friedman very much shared the outlook of Friedrich Hayek (joint Nobel Prize winner in 1974) whose trenchant Road to Serfdom (1944) he referred to as that "profound and influential book".

It was not until the realisation in academic and government circles that Keynesianism as it had been applied in the past was seriously flawed, that Friedman's star began to rise in the United Kingdom, although well before that time, economists on both sides of the Atlantic had been well aware that there was a Chicago School in the U.S.A. and that Milton Friedman, Professor of Economics at the University of Chicago, was its main protagonist.

Two events in 1976 gave a fillip to Friedmanite doctrines. Friedman himself received the Nobel Prize for Economics and Healey, Britain's Chancellor of the Exchequer at that time, promoted control of the money supply to be a major, though not yet dominant, strand in the country's economic policy. By the end of the decade, even greater obeisance was being made to the monetary factor by an influential section of the Conservative party. The beliefs of Sir Keith Joseph and the Centre for Policy Studies were becoming the new orthodoxy. More importantly, they were part and parcel of the conviction policies espoused by Margaret Thatcher and her immediate entourage.

By the end of the decade, monetarism was a familiar term in Britain, seized on by the right as something not yet tried on the troubled British economy and anathematised by the left as the progenitor of low wages, poor working conditions and unemployment. The Friedmanite view was that, though the medicine might be painful in the short run, in the long run it would promote a far higher degree of national wealth and well-being than could ever be achieved by constant meddling with market forces.

Hitherto, the accepted wisdom, especially as embodied in the workings of the Phillips Curve, and endorsed by common sense, was that inflation and unemployment must move in opposite directions; if inflation was high, unemployment would be low and vice versa. But Friedman pointed out that for a number of years, the opposite had been happening; unemployment and inflation had been rising together.

Friedman's explanation was this: at any one time there is a natural rate of unemployment. What this is would depend on the efficiency of the labour market. Where there are a few impediments to free movement of labour, either occupationally or geographically, this "natural rate" will be low; when monopolistic practices by employers or unions, minimum wage legislation or out-dated workshop rules impair the functioning of the labour market, then the natural rate of unemployment will be high and vice versa.

Pumping money into an economy in which unemployment is already down to its natural level simply leads - after an initial boost - to a loss of jobs. Slow growth and high unemployment are not cures for inflation but side effects. All that the government can do is to keep the money supply down and remove the obstacles to the efficient functioning of the labour market. Inflation was not caused by trade unions but by governments and their Central Banks, by allowing the money supply to outstrip the productive capacity of the country.

As a matter of historical fact, neither Keynesian demand management, nor monetary policy when rigorously applied, have produced satisfactory results in this country. The Barber boom, the ultimate in Keynesian expansionism, was an originating cause of the high price rises in the early Seventies, accentuated a year or two later by the increase in oil and commodity prices, whilst the obsessive adherence to monetary targets in the early years of the Thatcher government helped to foist on the country its highest ever unemployment level.

CHAPTER SIX
ACCEPTING THE UNACCEPTABLE

Well before the end of the war and increasingly after Alamein and Stalingrad, people began to give serious thought about what sort of a world it was going to be when the war was over. This was no academic exercise because they were well aware that the answer to that question would determine the well-being and happiness of themselves and their families for many years to come.

Hopes and fears were focused on a variety of topics. When focused on unemployment, they were somewhat schizoid. There was a general belief that once the backlog of orders accumulated during hostilities had been made good, unemployment would shoot up as it had done in 1920. At the same time, the view was widely expressed that people 'wouldn't stand for it again'. Exactly what form this refusal to stand for it would take was usually left rather vague. It is probably true that whilst few people had in mind the overthrow of the government by coup d'etat or violence, the least they expected was the downfall by ballot of any government so inept as to let it happen.

But, as already noted, at the 1983 election, though even the official count of unemployment was in excess of three million, the Conservatives were re-elected with a majority increased from 43 to 144. How did this extraordinary volte-face in public opinion come about?

An Ideal Demoted.

In the early post-war years, full employment was seen as the logical consequence of the huge backlog which had accumulated during the war years in building, manufacture and the basic services. As the immediate post-war years receded and jobs remained plentiful, people began to hope and even believe that full employment had come to stay. New-fangled Keynesian techniques, continuing high expenditure on defence and welfare, plus a limited measure of income redistribution, had combined to create an aggregate demand for labour which would provide jobs for virtually the whole work force.

This optimism about the future of unemployment was reflected in C.A.R. Crosland's highly influential book, The Future of Socialism, published in 1956. Britain, he held, was now enjoying the benefits of a new sort of capitalism, conditioned if not created by the greater powers in the hands of workers as a result of full employment. The economic problem had been solved, paradoxically perhaps, under the Conservatives. Labour, if they were to regain power, must throw away "the much thumbed guide books of the past", and concentrate on social objectives, such as greater equality and improving the quality of life.

Crosland was wrong in his assumption that full employment had come to stay, though right when he observed "the years ahead are more likely to be characterised by inflation than unemployment".

By the mid-Fifties, the government too were becoming very conscious of the upward pressure on prices which full employment seemed to be generating. In the hope of increasing public awareness of this problem, they published in the same year as Crosland's The Future of Socialism a White Paper (Cmnd 9725) entitled, 'The Economic Implications of Full Employment'.

In a brief history of events since 1945, the White Paper pointed out that UK prices in that period had risen by about 50%, most of this rise being due to domestic costs of production rather than increases in the price of imports. If this trend continued, Britain would find it increasingly difficult to compete in international markets with consequent detriment to employment and the standard of living. The future, therefore, might be one not of full employment and inflation, but of full employment or inflation.

The government hoped that greater awareness of the nature of the problem would contribute to a solution and to that end, in July 1957, announced the formation of a Council on Prices, Productivity and Incomes. The Council was to consist of three eminent persons - hence the title, the 'Three Wise Men' - a Law Lord (Lord Cohen), an accountant and an economist.

The government were anxious to avoid any impression that they were looking for some prestigious body to sanction resort to unemployment as a remedy for inflation. Hence the wording of the Council's terms of reference: "Having regard to the desirability of full employment and increasing standards of life based on expanding production and reasonable stability in prices, to keep under review changes in prices, productivity and the level of incomes (including wages, salaries and profits) and to report from time to time."

This injunction did not deter the Council from concluding in its first report, issued in March 1958, with these words: "The percentage of unemployment has risen only from 1.2% in January 1956 to 1.8% in January 1958. It would not be alarming if it were somewhat higher."

Such a pronouncement was more than enough to condemn the Council in the eyes of the TUC, always strident in its horror of unemployment (but often lukewarm about countermeasures which might injure the sacred cow of free collective bargaining).

Whilst the Three Wise Men were cogitating a wider discussion was taking place about the causes of inflation. Some held that it was mainly a "demand-pull", others that it was mainly a "cost-push" phenomenon. The "demand-pull" champions held that once full employment had been attained, any extra demand led not to more jobs but to higher inflation. The "cost-push" champions believed that there were many factors which raised costs independently of the state of demand, notably when trade unions negotiated wage rises in excess of productivity increases or when external factors, such as the Korean war commodity boom, raised the price of imports.

From November 1958 onwards, contestants had a new and more

meaty bone to bite on. This was the phenomenon which became known as the "Phillips curve". In the edition of Economica for that month, Professor Phillips published an article entitled, The Relation between Unemployment and the Rate of Change of Money Wage Rates in the United Kingdom 1861-1957. The conclusion he drew from his statistics was that for nearly a hundred years there had been a tendency for the rate of change in money wages to be high when unemployment was low and to be low or even negative when unemployment was high.

Professor Phillips had plotted his figures on a graph (hence the "Phillips curve") and commentators noted that if for any given rate of wage increases there was a higher rate of unemployment, the curve "shifted to the right", if there was a lower rate of unemployment for a given wage rate it "shifted to the left". The glut of comment and prognostication let loose by the Phillips Curve reinforced the view that there was a trade-off between full employment and stable prices; the country could enjoy one or the other, but not both at the same time.

In later years, as unemployment, wages and prices rose in unison, it became difficult to accept the Phillips Curve thesis except in a far more sophisticated form that at first mooted.

Academics were more free than politicians to call into question the sanctity of full employment and in the late Fifties and early Sixties, there was a large body of opinion in the universities and research institutes advocating that the economy be run with rather more spare capacity of both capital and labour. A leading advocate of this view was Professor Paish of the London School of Economics who, in his Studies in an Inflationary Economy (1962), and elsewhere, argued that if Britain was to prevent a continuing balance of payments crisis, she must accept a permanent unemployment level of 500,000 or a little bit over 2%. Twenty years later, such a level would be regarded as Utopian; in the early Sixties it sounded rather shocking.

The Thorneycroft resignations in 1958 drew public attention to the difficulties of reconciling full employment with stable prices. But during the last years of Conservative rule, the 1962-63 recession, hopes of what the newly established National Economic Development Council might achieve and, in 1964, the imminence of a general election, all helped to muffle any sounds which might be interpreted as casting doubts on the sanctity of full employment. Both Labour and Conservative politicians were well aware that the warnings about excessive wage claims given by Keynes, Beveridge and governments in their White Papers of 1944 and 1956, were not idle warnings. But the Conservatives did not wish to jeopardise, especially in election years, their remarkable record on unemployment whilst the last thing Labour leaders were ready to do was to start berating the trade unions, the very organisations which sustained them in funds and in votes.

Across the Atlantic, winds were gathering which would soon carry across to these islands the allurements (to certain minds) of monetarism. Emerging from the complexities of the monetarist doctrine was the message that responsibility for excessive price rises and their concomitant unemployment, lay not with greedy trade unions over-reaching themselves but with foolish governments for allowing the money supply to get out of hand. But in 1964, both the word and its connotation were virtually unknown in this country.

As year succeeded year, however, without any return to the unemployment experienced in the inter-war years, the belief became entrenched that modern governments both could and should maintain full employment. In the 'recession' of 1958-59, unemployment never rose above 2.1% and in that of 1962-63, never above 2.4%. So much had expectations been raised by time and good fortune that the Beveridge 3%, which had seemed so chimerical when first put forward, now seemed unacceptably high - and positively dangerous for whatever government was in power.

Indeed, Samuel Brittan, in his book, Steering the Economy (Penguin 1971), noted that during most of the 1950s and 1960s, Chancellors behaved like Pavlovian dogs, responding to two main stimuli; one was "a run on the reserves" and the other was "500,000 unemployed" - a figure which was later increased to above 600,000. On the whole (although not invariably), it was the officials who became alarmed on the first stimulus and ministers on the second, although each side usually managed to communicate its alarm to the other.

Nevertheless, although all parties continued to proclaim their dedication to full employment, the actual level of unemployment in the Sixties was quite a little higher than in the Fifties. There was less condemnation of the Paish thesis that a little more slack in the labour market was necessary if Britain was to master her balance of payments problems. The ceiling of acceptability also seemed to be raised when Harold Wilson, after outlining his economy proposals to the House of Commons in July 1966, indicated that he expected the level of unemployment to rise from "about 1 1/2% to between 1 1/2% to 2%. Naturally the draconian measures of that year came in for a lot of criticism but neither the disgruntled left wing of his own party nor the various opposition spokesmen specially picked on the expected rise in unemployment as their main grounds of criticism.

The only real public uproar on account of unemployment occurred in 1971-72 when the total very briefly rose to more than one million and debates in Parliament were matched outside by rallies, protest meetings and demonstrations. As the heat of acrimony rose, the government became badly rattled. The post-war consensus about full employment had not yet begun to crumble and the dispute between the two main parties was not about whether but about how unemployment should be brought down. The government's reply to criticism was the ill-fated 'Barber boom'.

The reaction to ever higher and more prolonged unemployment which occurred under the Labour government which followed, was completely different, although by mid 1976, the total exceeded one and a half million. This state of affairs did not go without comment and criticism, especially from Labour's own left wing, but compared with the protests which unemployment on a much smaller scale had evoked under the Heath government, the reaction was mild. It was not the level of unemployment which doomed the 1974-79 Labour government but the offence they had given to so many of their own supporters by their incomes policy and the anger which so many people felt because of the strikes and demonstrations by public service workers in the Winter of Discontent.

Joel Barnett, Chief Secretary to the Treasury 1974-79, calls attention to this paradox in his Inside the Treasury (A. Deutsch 1982). "If," he wrote, "anybody had told us in 1974 that we in a Labour government would preside over [unemployment] levels of that size we would have derided them. But not only did we do so for many years and despite criticisms from the union movement and our activists inside and outside the House of Commons, we did so with comparatively little trouble. I do not recall a single letter in the whole of that time complaining specifically about this terribly high level of unemployment. I know by talking to other Ministers and backbenchers that the same quietist mood applied in their constituencies."

Public protest at very much higher unemployment was even more muted under the Thatcher government. As the total rose from 1,300,000 to 3,000,000 during her first Ministry, the workers were too numbed, the trade unions too cowed and the Labour opposition too distracted by its own internal quarrels to mount any serious campaign against unemployment. Moreover, many people welcomed the new regime which brought with it the benefactions of lower income tax and few regulations; best of all, its hands seemed almost to be grasping the holy Grail of low inflation. Few would profess that unemployment was a "good thing" but many averred with approval that it was helping to bring down British labour costs which were such a handicap to her in her export markets.

It would be wrong, however, to conclude that unemployment had ceased altogether to be a political issue. In the 1979 election, the Conservatives' poster, "Labour Isn't Working", was undoubtedly a very effective one - however ironic in the light of what was soon to happen under a Conservative government. Moreover, in the 1983 election in the 100 constituencies which had recently recorded the highest level of unemployment, the Conservatives won only one and in the 100 which had recorded the lowest rate, Labour won none at all.

In other words, unemployment had been demoted but not defused as a political issue. Both the Labour government of 1974-79 and the Conservative administration which followed it reconciled themselves to a high level of unemployment in the belief that to do otherwise would wreck their anti-inflation policies.

Nevertheless, as the figures in the Conservatives' first year of office passed the high peak reached under Labour the number of people, according to Gallup, who saw unemployment as the most urgent problem facing the country rose from 23% in May to 49% in July. By the time of the 1983 general election, the tally of unemployed had virtually doubled to over 3 million. How is it that, despite this horrendous total, there was no general rising up of the population to say, 'No, the misery and impoverishment of so many of our fellow-citizens is not a price we are prepared to pay'?

To answer this question one has to remember that even in the worst of times the unemployed are only a minority of the population - the long-term unemployed even a smaller proportion - so that to have been effective any such uprising in public opinion would have required the support of both the unemployed and a goodly section of the general public. Why was this not forthcoming?

The Unemployed Have Not the "Clout".

Reference is often made to the "pool of unemployed". This metaphor is apposite enough so long as it is recognised that it is not a static pool. Each month some 300,000 or more men and women in UK move into and a similar number move out of this "pool". When the economy is expanding the "exits" exceed the "entrants"; when it is contracting the reverse holds true. Between those who have just entered the pool and those heading steadily or speedily for the exit are the ones who are slow-moving or even static, i.e. the long-term unemployed.

Some of those speeding successfully for the exits will have been made redundant not for any personal shortcomings but because of structural change in their industry or because their firm has been taken over by some other company. Prominent amongst these will be the professionally qualified, the managers, the entrepreneurs, the energetic and the articulate, just the sort of workers well placed to find a new employer. There will be others who, though not so eminently "marketable" as these, are in no serious danger of being long without a job.

Few of these will identify with the unemployed; most will have found the experience of being 'on the dole' distasteful and though sympathetic to the 'genuine' unemployed in a vague sort of way, will have no wish to involve themselves politically or otherwise on their behalf.

What is left after these categories have been eliminated is a residue of long-term unemployed, largely though not exclusively composed of the elderly, the disabled, those with poor educational qualifications and ethnic minorities. A large number of these remnants suffer the additional disadvantage of living in job-starved inner cities, in the less salubrious suburbs or in one of the high unemployment regions.

Accumulated evidence shows that long-term unemployment is a timeless phenomenon, just as detrimental in its effects on the individual in the Nineties as it was in the inter-war years. Anyone wanting to assess these effects need not go short of literature on the subject. Two (amongst many) specially revealing studies are the Pilgrim Trust's Men Without Work (1938) and the Manpower Services Commission's Study of the Long-Term Unemployed (1980). The malign effects of long-term unemployment vary in pattern and severity, but a typical sequence of events is as follows.

The initial mood on being made redundant is one of shock. But the victim soon recovers his equanimity and a mood of optimism ensues, especially if he has a good employment record, a recognised skill or a few friends who might put him on to something. Often this optimism is justified, but when successive efforts to find work come to naught this gives way to pessimism. Is it surprising if, by this time, his self-confidence sapped by numerous rebuffs, the enthusiasm with which he conducts his job search begins to flag and listlessness and boredom set in? Is it surprising that he begins to feel an outcast from society?

This process of demoralisation is hastened and intensified by the practice followed by nearly all employers when engaging labour of giving preference to those with 'good employment records', which means amongst other things, not having been out of work for any length of time. This practice, unfortunate though it is for the unemployed, is understandable. A worker who has not worked for a considerable time inevitably begins to get out of touch with the latest developments in his trade, whilst the exigencies of living on a meagre income makes it difficult to maintain the smart appearance so desirable when applying for a job.

Suffusing all the comings and goings of the long-term unemployed are financial worries. It is not so bad to begin with, especially for those who have drawn a reasonably generous redundancy payment from state and employer - although these are not nearly so munificent or so widespread as is sometimes supposed. But as time goes by, clothes grow shabby, household appliances wear out and parents find themselves less and less able to provide their children with the sort of things which the parents of those in safe jobs purchase without thinking twice about it.

Money troubles are often the source of family tension and family quarrels break out where peace has reigned before. Nor does it always work out well when the former breadwinner becomes the "house person" whilst his wife goes out to work.

Health too becomes a problem. A considerable amount of research from the Pilgrim Trust onwards has established that the health of the unemployed is worse than that of the employed population. This is not surprising. Unless inhibited by collective agreements which prescribe the order of discharge most employers when trimming their labour forces, will first get rid of those with poor attendance records, notably the chronically sick. To that extent, sickness is certainly a cause of unemployment. It is also an effect of unemployment as those who lack the stimulus of regular work, who are beset by boredom and money worries and are probably subsisting on a poor diet, are obviously not on the road to healthy living.

It is clear that the composition of the unemployment registers and the effects of long-term unemployment together militate against the formation from amongst the unemployed themselves of any effective 'resistance movement' against the employment policies of the government of the day. Even if the desire to be effective is there, poverty, that imperious begetter of impotence, imposes severe restraints. How can one play an active part in any of society's myriad activities when even the purchase of a cup of coffee or a glass of beer can badly damage the weekly budget?

Public Attitude to Unemployment.

Had public repugnance to unemployment been as strong in 1983 as it was for at least twenty-five years after the war Labour, for all its disarray, would have toppled their opponents at the general election or, at the least, Labour-cum-Alliance voters would have done so. It is history that this did not happen.

Out by the 1980s was the doctrine that governments had failed if they could not provide work for virtually all their citizens of working age; in was the doctrine that a government had failed if it could not control inflation.

What the workforce were being told was that there was a market clearing price for labour and if, through trade union or other pressures, they set the supply price of their labour above this level then some of them would be left without jobs. For every economy, the argument went there is a "natural rate of unemployment", a concept later elaborated to a 'non-accelerating inflation rate of unemployment (NAIRU)'. It was left to non-governmental voices to note how close was the affinity between this doctrine and the Marxist thesis that capitalism functioned as it did because of a 'reserve army of unemployed' to be hired or fired according to fluctuations in trade.

The average voter may not have thought in these abstractions but, having witnessed the distortions and anomalies which arose from the regulatory strivings of the Wilson, Heath and Callaghan regimes, he was much more receptive to laudations of the market economy than he otherwise might have been.

The part which economic fact and economic theory played in reconciling the public to a level of unemployment they would have regarded as appalling in earlier times, was strongly reinforced by the consequences of several decades of social change. In the 1930s, there was an affinity which no longer existed in the Eighties, between the unemployed and the broad mass of employees. Both the class system and the economic system of the day bonded them together. Where unemployment was high, it was regarded as a community disaster and those less directly affected would endeavour to sustain the morale of the unemployed and give whatever material assistance they could to the families most in need. In the 1980s, closure of a mine or factory was still regarded as a community disaster but there was much more of a 'sauve qui peut' attitude abroad. Although there were several marches of the unemployed in the early Eighties, none of them aroused nationwide sympathy as the Jarrow March of 1936 had done.

This absence of working class solidarity stemmed in part from the changes which had taken place in the occupational structure of society. Forty years after the war, neither agriculture nor manufacturing, nor the greatly expanded service industries, any longer had need of those masses of semi-skilled and unskilled workers who were the infantrymen of the old Labour Movement. Some of those who in earlier years would have been part of the low or no wage proletariat had, by better education, better training or better luck, found their way to jobs in factory, farming or office which enabled them to enjoy a lifestyle quite different from those subsisting on the pittance of welfare payments. Many of them too had sons or daughters who, through higher education and their own exertions, had made their way to managerial or professional jobs. There had, in fact, been a substantial migration into the world of the bourgeoisie.

Jobs requiring little or no skill had not disappeared altogether, but they existed in far fewer numbers. Many of them were purely temporary, reflecting the seasonal demands of Christmas or the summer holiday period. Others were unattractive in pay or working conditions or both, so that staff turnover was high. Those who took such jobs were not included amongst the long-term unemployed as usually defined, i.e. 52 continuous weeks without employment, but the problems they faced were very similar and the influence they exerted on government just as nugatory.

In themselves these occupational changes were on balance pleasing to those who believed that British class divisions had been too segregative and jarring in the past. The losers had been the long-term unemployed who found former allies turned, at the best, into lukewarm supporters. Even if working in unison they had insufficient "clout" to matter much to the government in power.

But what about the always numerous, often influential, sectors of society which lay outside these categories? Would their censures shame the government into modifying or even reversing its employment policy?

Let us put the clock back to the end of the war years. No doubt many of those who foretold death and destruction for any government which allowed unemployment to swell to 1920s and 1930s' proportions, had in mind dole queues very different in composition from those of the Eighties. When the post-World War One depression set in, ex-servicemen who had borne the brunt of the fighting on the Western Front and elsewhere, were conspicuous among the unemployed. Moreover, in those days the comings and goings of the unemployed were far more visible as benefit was paid in cash and signing on rules were stricter.

As World War Two drew to its close, most adults could recall those days and had visions of a similar fate befalling those who had fought on various fronts in this war. As we have seen when mass unemployment did return, the long-term registers were mainly composed of people very different in calibre and background and far less likely to evoke the sympathies of the prospering majority.

Again, social factors were intertwined with the imperatives of economics. In the 1920s (and to a diminishing extent in the 1930s), a family of any standing in the community would have at least one maid, probably living in, a gardener, whole or part-time and perhaps a chauffeur-handyman. From these the head of the household (as the male was always regarded) and even more his wife would learn quite a bit about the families of those they employed, their hopes, their fears, their idiosyncrasies. Two car families were a rarity and middle class housewives would often chat to working class women at the bus or tram stop or whilst on their journeys.

By the 1980s few women stayed at home all day, even fewer had servants whilst two cars to a family was no longer a sign of exceptional wealth. Although unemployment caused anxiety and concern in a few middle class families, their haunts and their homes were in general free from the miasma of depression which pervaded the inner cities and the more down-at-heel suburbs. Physically only a mile or two apart, in lifestyle, in ethos and in outlook they were worlds away from each other.

Sympathy does not flourish where there is no empathy and the conclusion it seemed obvious to draw from the 1983 election was that full employment was a feature of a now vanishing past or a very distant future. It was still an ideal, but now an unrealisable one.

'The Right to Work.'

There is no doubt that the resolve of the Thatcher and Major governments to make the reduction in inflation a top priority had widespread popular support. In this aim they were eventually successful, but the price paid was a huge increase in unemployment from 1,299,000 at the time of the May 1979 election to 3,408,000 in June 1986. (These are official figures and, as is generally recognised, they seriously understate reality.) After that the fall in unemployment was - for a time - almost as dramatic as its previous rise, bringing the total down to 1,556,000 in June 1990. This recovery was short-lived. At the first whiff of recession the figures shot up again and were almost back to three million by the end of 1993.

The official reaction to this situation is - keep inflation down, get the economy expanding and jobs will accrue. This is only a half truth. New jobs will certainly appear once the economy expands but orthodox economic growth will never reduce unemployment to a satisfactory level let alone to the Beveridge 3%. It also has to be remembered that when economic growth does take place, much of it is normally achieved by the substitution of machines for human labour.

If present policies prevail, the grim prospect for the future is one of alternations between high unemployment and mass unemployment. In either situation there will remain an underclass in part apathetic, in part rebellious and in part violent, shut out from the activities and amenities enjoyed by the rest of the community. The young will be prominent in this underclass but well represented, also will be those men and women too easily forgotten who still have 10-15 years to go before retirement, but who, because of their age, are so often spurned by employers.

Anyone who thinks that there is an easy solution to the unemployment problem is either a simpleton or a quack. Yet finding a solution is as much a matter of political will as intellectual acumen. If the British government knew that the existence of one million unemployed would put them on probation and two million would carry a death sentence so far as voters were concerned, it would concentrate their minds wondrously towards finding a solution.

Amid the rubble of discarded theories and disappointed hopes one thing stands out clearly. To restore full employment or anything like full employment the demand side of the labour market must be strengthened. This means that central and local government, directly and indirectly will have to create jobs. This will be anathema to the hard-line devotees of the free market but by no other means can the surplus labour be absorbed into a useful role in society.

It is commendable for any government to improve the supply side of the labour market so long as it is done by better education and training and not by whittling away workers' rights and safeguards under the euphemism of 'deregulation'. But hope turns into let-down if there is no demand for the skills and competence the trainee has acquired.

Of course there is the danger that as unemployment declines inflationary pressures will build up again. But surely we have learnt some lessons from the past and could now do more to nip it in the bud than we managed last time round. It is also reasonable to hope that nothing as damaging as the huge oil price rises of the early seventies and early eighties will be repeated.

The argument can also be put forward that we live less and less in a closed community and that what happens here is determined by what happens in Brussels, Washington, Tokyo or elsewhere. That is so but the contrary is also true, that if we play a constructive role in the new Europe our power to influence events will be far greater than it would be in a less integrated community.

At the moment of writing there are roughly 2 3/4 million unemployed. The national wealth and welfare would be notably augmented if, say, 2 million of this number were transformed from an idle to an active workforce. Such an achievement would not only be in tune with the supposed British belief in fair play; it would also accord with article 23 of the United Nations Universal Declaration of Human Rights, viz 'Everyone has the right to work, to free choice of employment, to just and favourable conditions of work and to protection against unemployment'.

APPENDIX ONE
SOME PRINCIPAL MINISTERS, 1945 - 1983

PRIME MINISTERS	CHANCELLORS OF THE EXCHEQUER	
Clement Attlee, July 45 - Oct 51	Hugh Dalton	July 45 - Nov 47
	Stafford Cripps	Nov 47 - Oct 50
	Hugh Gaitskell	Oct 50 - Oct 51
Winston Churchill Oct 51 - April 55	Robert Butler	Oct 51 - Dec 55
Anthony Eden April 55 - Jan 57	Harold Macmillan	Dec 55 - Jan 57
Harold Macmillan Jan 57 - Oct 63	Peter Thorneycroft	Jan 57 - Jan 58
	Derick Heathcoat-Amory	Jan 58 - July 60
	Selwyn Lloyd	July 60 - July 62
Alec Douglas-Home Oct 63 - Oct 64	Reginald Maudling	July 62 - Oct 64
Harold Wilson Oct 64 - June 70	James Callaghan	Oct 64 - Nov 67
	Roy Jenkins	Nov 67 - June 70
Edward Heath June 70 - Feb 74	Iain Macleod	June 70 - July 70
	Anthony Barber	July 70 - Feb 74
Harold Wilson Feb 74 - April 76	Denis Healey	Feb 74 - May 79
	Geoffrey Howe	May 79 - June 83
James Callaghan April 76 - May 79		
Margaret Thatcher May 79 - June 83	Geoffrey Howe	May 79 - June 83

MINISTERS OF LABOUR & NATIONAL SERVICE

George Isaacs	August 45 - Jan 51
Arthur Robens	Jan 51 - Oct 51
Walter Monckton	Oct 51 - Dec 55
Iain Macleod	Dec 55 - Oct 59
Edward Heath	Oct 59 - July 60
	National Service dropped from title in Nov 59
John Hare	July 60 - Oct 63
John Godber	Oct 63 - Oct 64
Roy Gunter	Oct 64 - April 68

SECRETARIES OF STATE FOR EMPLOYMENT AND PRODUCTIVITY

Barbara Castle	April 68 - June 70
Robert Carr	June 70 - April 72
	Productivity dropped from title in Nov 70
Maurice Macmillan	April 72 - Dec 73
William Whitelaw	Dec 73 - Feb 74
Michael Foot	March 74 - April 76
Albert Booth	April 76 - May 79
James Prior	May 79 - Sept 81
Norman Tebbit	Sept 81 - Oct 83

APPENDIX TWO
STATISTICS

Although statistics are an essential ingredient of any meaningful study of unemployment, I do not wish to lead my readers into a jungle of figures which will obscure rather than clarify the human problems of unemployment. I hope, therefore, that the figures I have chosen to include in this Appendix will neither overfeed nor undernourish their appetite for pabulum of this sort.

To understand what the above Tables at the beginning of each chapter signify, the following points should be noted. The first column, as is self-evident, simply indicates the year to which each (horizontal) line of statistics refers.

The second column indicates the "Recorded Monthly Total" or 'Head Count' of unemployed averaged over the whole year and unvaried by any seasonal adjustment. (I believe that 'head count' conveys its meaning more accurately than any other term and this is the one I have put at the head of the column and used, as appropriate, in the text.)

The third column shows the number of unemployed as a percentage of all employees averaged over the whole year after adjustments have been made for seasonal factors. The object of eliminating seasonal factors is to establish a trend, something which can only be done if the figures used have been compiled on a uniform basis. The largest of these seasonal factors is the influx of school leavers after the summer term. Other examples of seasonal factors are the extra employees taken on in summer to deal with the tourist and holiday trade, the dismissal during January of staff taken on to cope with Christmas shopping and the New Year Sales, and the decline in winter of jobs in building and other outdoor activities, especially when the weather is severe.

These seasonally adjusted figures provide essential data for the Treasury and non-governmental organisations when constructing the models now deemed essential for economic forecasting and the formulation of policy.

The fourth column of statistics shows the number of long-term unemployed, a term which is usually, as here, taken to denote those who have been out of work continuously for more than 52 weeks.

The Department of Employment's practice has been to publish these figures once a quarter but not to average them out over the whole year. I have, therefore, selected the figures for October, a month when seasonal distortions are slight.

The fifth and last line of figures (Unfilled Vacancies) refers to vacancies which have been notified to the official employment agencies and were unfilled on the day of the count. By 'official' is meant in the earlier years the Employment Exchanges and Youth Employment Offices, in the later years Job Centres and Careers Offices. It is usually estimated that the official agencies are notified of about one third of the total of job vacancies which have occurred, the proportion being rather higher for manual and rather lower for white collar jobs. As with the long-term unemployed, the October figure for each year has been used.

As noted earlier (see p 15), one effect of the 1946 National Insurance Act was to extend the coverage and improve the accuracy of the unemployment statistics. For nearly 20 years, following the Act, little was done to probe what went on behind this statistical veil. The unemployment statistics were regarded mainly as a weather vane, indicating that expansionary measures were needed if the national total exceeded half a million and measures of the opposite sort if they fell too far below that figure.

The Labour government came to power in 1964 convinced that it could improve on the Conservatives' record of economic growth.

This goal would not be achieved without a considerable redeployment of labour from inessential and declining industries to new and expanding ones. To ensure that workers found the jobs and employers the employees that would bring this about, it would be necessary to improve the workings of the labour market. The country could not afford nor should individuals have to endure long periods of idleness simply because employers and employees were ignorant of each other's needs and whereabouts.

Hopes so blithely held of record-breaking expansion soon faded and by the summer of 1966, the government was subordinating economic growth to the protection of sterling and righting the balance of payments.

Economic, like military efficiency, demands good intelligence and steps were taken to improve the range and accuracy of statistical information at national, regional and local level. Despite this cornucopia of figures the riddle stayed unanswered of how far they represented a real labour reserve and how far an enumeration of a problem which was social rather than economic.

The question of what these statistics really meant came very much to the fore when unemployment shot up to over a million during the 1970-74 Conservative government. In order to shed light on the problem, the Prime Minister appointed a Working Party of officials to look into the matter and report. The nature of the problem can best be understood by quoting in full their terms of reference, viz: "To consider whether the statistics which are at present collected relating to the registered unemployed, and others in the population of working age who are neither in employment nor registered as unemployed, need to be further subdivided, supplemented or presented differently in order to provide a more accurate indication of the real level of unused labour resources in the economy."

Those who questioned the validity of the unemployment figures did so from opposite poles. From one pole came the criticism that the figures included several categories who were not genuinely unemployed, such as men and women briefly in transit from job to job, those who were on the verge of retirement and "the unemployables". From the opposite poles came the counterblast that the figures excluded certain categories who genuinely wanted work, such as retirement pensioners who would derive no financial advantage from registering and, most notably, the many thousands of married women debarred from benefit because they had earlier exercised their option not to pay national insurance contributions.

In November 1972, the Working Party rendered their Report in the form of a White Paper (Cmnd 5157). They recommended few changes either in the compilation or coverage of the unemployment statistics. They rejected the idea of excluding the unemployables on the grounds that "difficulties of definition are such as to make the proposition administratively impracticable". Similar considerations induced them to rule out the idea of excluding those "not genuinely seeking work".

The only category whose treatment in the statistics they felt should be treated differently were the Temporarily Stopped. These, they recommended, should be excluded from the total of registered unemployed but published as a separate item in the monthly Press Notice, a recommendation which was implemented a few months later. Following this minor change, the compilation and coverage of the unemployment statistics remained virtually unaltered until almost the end of the decade.

The advent of a Conservative government in 1979 marked the beginning of a succession of changes almost all of which had the effect of reducing the number of those officially recognised as being unemployed. The nature of those changes to the end of 1983 are listed in following Table for use of which I am indebted to the Unemployment Unit.

DATE	CHANGE ESTIMATED EFFECT ON MONTHLY COUNT	
Oct 1979	Change to fortnightly payment of benefits	+ 20,000
Oct 1979	Compensating downward adjustment to published seasonally adjusted totals	- 20,000
Feb 1981	First published estimate of register effect of special employment and training measures (coverage increased from 250,000 participants at start of 1979 to 668,000 by Jan 1986.)	- 370,000 (-495,000 Jan 1986)
July to Oct 1981	Seasonally adjusted figures for these months reduced by 20,000 to compensate for effect on count of emergency procedures to deal with DHSS industrial action.	- 20,000
July 1981	Unemployed men aged 60 and above, drawing supplementary benefit for a year by or more given option of long-term rate in return for not registering for work.	- 30,000 by May 1982
July 1982	Taxation of Unemployment Benefit. Suggested that this might have reduced count by encouraging	

single parents to switch to
(untaxed) supplementary   no estimate
benefit.   available

Oct 1982   Change in definition and compilation
                        of monthly unemployment figures
                        from a clerical count of people
                        registered for work at Jobcentres
                        and careers offices to a computer
                        count covering only benefit
                        claimants. (In addition,
                        the estimated effect on   -170,000 to
                        the number of school   -190,000
                        leavers recorded.)   -26,000

Oct 1982   Monthly publication of number of
                        unemployed people seeking part-time
                        work (less than 30 hours a week)
                        discontinued.
                        Final figure - for September 1982 - 52,204

April 1983   Men aged 60 and over and not
                        entitled to benefit no longer
                        required to sign   -107,400 by
                        on at benefit offices in
                        order to get   June 1983
                        NI credits.

June 1983   All men aged 60 and over
                        allowed long term rate
                        supplementary benefit rate
                        as soon as they come onto   - 54,400 by
                        supplementary benefit.   June 1983

June 1983   As a result of provision introduced in
                        November 1980 barring school leavers

from claiming benefit until
September each year,
together with change in
monthly count to claimants
only in October 1982
unemployed school-leavers
are missed from the
monthly figures for June,   -100,000 to
July and August each year.   - 200,000

The main object of these changes was to reduce the published figure of unemployed by excluding certain categories of the workless from the official count - notwithstanding the fact that they had not ceased in fact to be unemployed. The largest and most blatant example of this was the exclusion of those on Special Employment Schemes; since being unemployed was a basic condition of acceptance for such Schemes, it is difficult to defend this exclusion on grounds of either logic or equity.

The political motive for trying to make the official figures less gruesome than the reality is too obvious to need elaborating, although those with a genuine interest in or concern about the unemployed were not taken in by this statistical derring-do.

UNEMPLOYMENT AND VACANCIES, 1945 -70, GREAT BRITAIN

| | UNEMPLOYMENT | | VACANCIES | |
	(a) Head Count by thousands	(b) Percentage	(c) Long-term*	(d) Unfilled Vacancies
1945	140.5	1.3	-	-
1946	363.1	2.5	-	-
1947	468.3	3.1	-	-
1948	310.0	1.5	39.9	401.1
1949	308.0	1.5	36.9	366.7
1950	314.2	1.5	35.9	353.7
1951	252.9	1.1	27.3	410.5
1952	414.2	1.6	28.7	249.7
1953	340.0	1.5	33.3	282.6
1954	282.8	1.2	27.9	348.0
1955	252.2	1.0	21.9	424.2
1956	257.0	1.0	21.0	334.4
1957	312.5	1.3	27.8	283.7
1958	457.4	1.9	38.7	178.8
1959	475.2	2.0	60.7	255.1
1960	360.4	1.5	55.3	337.4
1961	340.7	1.3	46.9	328.1
1962	463.2	1.8	57.3	200.5
1963	573.2	2.2	77.1	213.9
1964	380.6	1.6	63.2	334.8
1965	328.8	1.3	51.1	372.5
1966	359.7	1.4	48.0	301.3
1967	519.0	2.2	72.3	241.1
1968	546.9	2.4	88.4	267.8
1969	539.3	2.3	95.5	271.8
1970	576.8	2.5	101.7	244.3

* Long-term - i.e. over 52 weeks

(a) not seasonally adjusted
(b) seasonally adjusted
(c) October figures
(d) October figures.

Source: British Labour Statistics, Historical Abstract, 1886-1968
        Employment Gazette

UNEMPLOYMENT AND VACANCIES, 1970-1991, UNITED KINGDOM

	UNEMPLOYMENT		VACANCIES	
	(a) Head Count by thousands	(b) Percentage	(c) Long-term*	(d) Unfilled Vacancies
1970	612.2	2.5	101.7**	244.3 (61.6)**
1971	792.1	3.4	129.9**	159.2 (40.0)**
1972	875.6	3.7	177.6**	212.5 (46.6)**
1973	618.8	2.6	142.6**	486.3 (121.3)**
1974	614.9	2.6	127.7**	299.1 (76.5)**
1975	997.6	4.2	161.2	132.0 (26.4)
1976	1358.8	5.8	264.6	139.8 (23.3)
1977	1402.7	5.6	324.3	169.1 (19.3)
1978	1382.9	5.5	333.1	241.4 (29.7)
1979	1295.7	5.1	337.0	246.5 (28.7)
1980	1664.9	6.5	401.1	108.7 (7.9)
1981	2520.4	10.2	784.6	107.2 (5.4)
1982	2916.9	12.0	1169.6	120.3 (6.3)
1983	3104.7	10.8	1142.9	139.8 (8.2)
1984	3159.8	11.1	1276.9	175.7 (9.7)
1985	3271.2	11.3	1351.9	206.4 (12.8)
1986	3289.1	11.5	1341.0	261.1 (14.7)
1987	2953.4	10.1	1172.2	312.2 (23.1)
1988	2370.4	8.1	855.5	271.8 (30.6)
1989	1798.7	6.3	613.3	242.2 (26.9)
1990	1664.4	5.8	507.7	171.9 (15.4)
1991	2291.9	8.1	654.0	129.9 (7.5)

* Long-term - i.e. over 52 weeks
** Figures for Great Britain only

(a)not seasonally adjusted
(b)seasonally adjusted
(c)October figures. Youth figures in brackets. There is some overlap between adult and youth figures.

Source: British Labour Statistics, Historical Abstract, 1886-1968
Employment Gazette

REGIONAL UNEMPLOYMENT - YEARLY AVERAGES*

	S.E & E.Anglia		SW	W.Mids	E.Mids	YksHumbs	NW	North	Wales	S'land	GB	NIre	
1949	1.1		1.4	0.6	0.7		1.7	2.6	4.0	3.0	1.5	6.5	
1950	1.1		1.4	0.5	0.8		1.6	2.8	3.7	3.1	1.5	5.8	
1951	0.9		1.2	0.4	0.7		1.2	2.2	2.7	2.5	1.2	6.1	
1952	1.3		1.5	0.9	1.5		3.1	2.6	2.8	3.3	2.0	10.3	
1953	1.2		1.6	1.1	1.0		2.1	2.4	2.9	3.0	1.6	8.1	
1954	1.0		1.4	0.6	0.8		1.5	2.3	2.4	2.8	1.3	7.0	
1955	0.7		1.1	0.5	0.6		1.4	1.8	1.8	2.4	1.1	6.8	
1956	0.8		1.3	1.1	0.7		1.3	1.5	2.0	2.4	1.2	6.4	
1957	1.1		1.8	1.3	0.9		1.6	1.7	2.6	2.6	1.4	7.3	
1958	1.4		2.2	1.6	1.8		2.7	2.4	3.8	3.8	2.1	9.3	
1959	1.3		2.1	1.5	1.7		2.8	3.3	3.8	4.4	2.2	7.8	
1960	1.0		1.7	1.0	1.1		1.9	2.9	1.7	3.6	1.6	6.7	
1961	1.0		1.4	1.4	1.0		1.6	2.5	2.6	3.1	1.5	7.5	
1962	1.3		1.7	1.8	1.5		2.5	3.7	3.1	3.8	2.0	7.5	
1963	1.6		2.1	2.0	1.9		3.1	5.0	3.6	4.8	2.5	7.9	
1964	2.0		1.5	0.9	1.1		2.1	3.3	2.6	3.6	1.6	6.6	
1965	0.9	1.3	1.6	0.9	0.9	1.1	1.6	2.6	2.6	3.0	1.4	6.1	
1966	1.0	1.4	1.8	1.3	1.1	1.2	1.5	2.6	2.9	2.9	1.4	6.1	
1967	1.7	2.1	2.5	2.5	1.8	2.1	2.5	4.0	4.1	3.9	2.2	7.3	
1968	1.6	2.0	2.5	2.2	1.9	2.6	2.5	4.7	4.0	3.8	2.4	7.1	
1969	1.5	1.9	1.8	1.9	2.2	2.6	2.4	4.8	4.0	3.7	2.4	7.1	
1970	1.6	2.1	2.8	2.0	2.2	2.9	2.7	4.6	3.8	4.6	2.5	6.8	
1971	2.1	3.2	3.3	3.0	2.9	3.9	3.9	5.7	4.4	5.7	3.4	7.9	
1972	2.2	2.9	3.4	3.6	3.1	4.2	4.9	6.3	4.8	6.4	3.7	8.0	
1973	1.5	1.9	2.4	2.2	2.1	2.8	3.6	3.7	3.4	4.5	2.6	6.1	
1974	1.6	1.9	2.7	N/A	2.2	2.7	3.5	4.6	3.7	4.0	2.6	5.7	UK
1975	2.1	2.6	3.4	3.1	2.6	2.9	4.0	5.9	5.6	5.2	4.1	7.9	4.1
1976	3.1	3.5	4.7	4.3	3.6	3.9	5.1	7.5	7.4	7.0	5.6	10.3	5.7
1977	3.3	3.8	4.9	4.2	3.6	4.0	5.3	8.3	8.0	8.0	6.0	11.0	6.2
1978	4.2	5.0	6.5	5.6	5.0	6.0	7.5	8.8	8.4	8.2	6.0	11.5	6.1
1979	3.7	4.5	5.7	5.5	5.0	5.7	7.1	8.6	8.0	8.0	5.6	11.3	6.1
1980	4.2	5.3	6.4	7.3	6.1	7.3	8.5	10.4	9.4	9.1	7.3	12.8	7.4
1981	7.0	8.3	9.2	12.5	9.1	11.4	12.7	14.7	13.5	12.4	10.2	16.8	10.4
1982	8.5	9.7	10.6	14.7	10.9	13.2	14.7	16.5	15.4	14.0	11.9	18.7	12.1
1983	4.3	10.2	11.2	15.6	11.8	14.1	15.8	17.7	15.9	14.0	12.8	20.2	12.9
1984	8.4	8.7	9.7	14.1	10.9	12.9	14.5	17.0	14.2	13.8	11.5	18.0	11.7
1985	8.6	8.8	9.7	14.1	11.3	13.3	14.6	17.3	14.6	14.0	11.7	18.0	11.9

1986	8.7	9.0	9.9	12.0	10.7	12.2	14.6	16.4	14.7	14.5	11.7	18.1	11.8
1987	7.4	7.7	8.5	9.2	9.6	10.0	13.1	14.9	14.4	14.0	10.4	11.8	10.6
1988	5.5	5.4	7.2	9.4	7.5	9.8	10.9	13.0	10.0	11.6	8.2	15.8	8.5
1989	3.9	3.6	5.3	6.7	5.5	7.5	8.6	10.2	7.5	9.3	6.1	14.5	6.3
1990	4.0	3.7	5.6	6.0	5.1	6.8	7.7	8.9	6.6	8.0	5.6	13.3	5.8
1991	6.9	5.8	9.4	8.6	7.2	8.7	9.4	10.4	8.7	8.7	8.0	13.7	8.1

* Not seasonally adjusted

Source: British Labour Statistics, Historical Abstract, 1886-1988
Employment Gazette

BIBLIOGRAPHY

ALDCROFT, Derek H. (1984) Full Employment, Harvester Press

BEHARREL, Andy, (1992)Unemployment and Job Creation, Macmillan

BEVERIDGE, William H. (1944) Full Employment in a Free Society, George Allen & Unwin

Ed BLACKABY, F.T. (1978) British Economic Policy 1960-74, Cambridge University Press (N.I.E.S.R. Publications)

BLEANEY, Michael, (1985) The Rise & Fall of Keynesian Economics, Macmillan

BRITTAN, Samuel, (1971)Steering the Economy, Penguin Books

BRITTAN, Samuel (1988)A Restatement of Economic Liberalism, Macmillan

BROWN, A.J. & BURROWS, E.M. (1977) Regional Economic Problems, Allen & Unwin

BROWNING, Peter, (1986) The Treasury and Economic Performance, Longman

BRUCE-GARDYNE, Jack, (1984) Mrs. Thatcher's Final Administration, Macmillan

CAIRNCROSS, Alec, (1992) The British Economy since 1945, Blackwell

CASTLE, Barbara, (1980)Diaries 1974-76, Book Club Associates

CLARK, Andrew & LAYARD, Richard (1989) U.K. Unemployment, Heineman Educational

COATES, David & HILLARD, John, (1986)The Economic Decline of Modern Britain, Wheatsheaf Books Ltd

Ed CRAFTS, N.F.R. WOODWARD,N (1991)The British Economy since 1945, Oxford University Press

CROSLAND, A. (1956) The Future of Socialism, Jonathan Cape

CROSSMAN, Richard, (1979) The Crossman Diaries, 1964-70, Book Club Associates

CUTLER, Tony et al, (1986) Keynes, Beveridge & Beyond, Routledge & Kegan Paul Ltd

Ed DAMESICK, Peter & Regional Problems, WOOD, Peter (1987) Oxford University Press

DANIEL, W.W. (1990) The Unemployed Flow, Policy Studies Institute

DEACON, Alan & BRADSHAW, Jonathon (1983) Reserved for the Poor, Basil Blackwell & Martin Robinson

EATWELL, Roger (1979) The 1945-51 Labour Government, Batsford Academic

FIELD, Frank (1977) The Conscript Army, Routledge & Kegan Paul

Ed FINEMAN, Stephen (1987) Unemployment, Personal and Social Consequences, Tavistock Publications

FRIEDMAN, Milton (1980)Free to Choose, Pelican Books

FRIEDMAN, Milton, (1985)The Tyranny of the Status Quo, Pelican Books

FRIEND, Andrew & METCALF, Andy Slump City, Pluto Press, 1981

GARDNER, Nick (1987) Decade of Discontent, Basil Blackwell

GARRATY, John, (1978) Unemployment in History, Harper & Row

GLYNN, Sean, (1991) No Alternatives?, Faber and Faber

GORDON, Alan, (1988) The Crisis of Unemployment, Christopher Helm

HALL, Maximillian, (1983)Monetary Policy since 1971, Macmillan

HASLUCK, Chris, (1987)Urban Unemployment, Longman

Ed HENNESY, P. & SELDON, Arthur, (1987) Ruling Performance Basil Blackwell

HAWKINS, Kevin, (1979) Unemployment, Penguin Books

HIGGINS, Joan et al, (1983) Government & Urban Policy, Basil Blackwell

HOLMES, Martin, (1985) The Labour Government, 1974-79 Macmillan

HOLMES, Martin, (1985)The First Thatcher Government, 1979-1983, Harvester Press

HUGHES, James, J. & PERLMAN, R. (1984) The Economics of Unemployment Harvester Press

215

ILLICH, Ivan, (1978) The Right to Useful Employment, Martin Boyars Publishers Ltd

JAY, Douglas, (1986) Sterling, Oxford University Press

JONES, Russell, (1987) Wages & Economic Policy, Allen & Unwin

KAVANNAGH, Dennis, (9187) Thatcherism & British Politics, Oxford University Press

KAVANNAGH, Dennis & MORRIS, Peter (9189) Consensus Politics, Basil Blackwell

KEANE, John & OWENS, John (1986) After Full Employment Hutchinson

KEEGAN, William, (1984)Mrs Thatcher's Economic Experiment, Allen Lane

KELLNER, Peter, (1982)Slump '82, New Statesman

KEYNES, J.M., (1936) The General Theory of Employment, Interest & Money, Macmillan

LAYARD, Richard, (1982) More Jobs, Less Inflation, Grant McIntyre

LAYARD, Richard, & PHILPOTT, John (1991) Stopping Unemployment, Employment Institute

Ed MACLENAN, Duncan & PARR, John b. (1979) Regional Policy, Martin Robertson

MADGWICK, P.J., STEEDS, D. & WILLIAMS,L.J. (1982) Britain since 1945, Hutchinson

Ed MAUNDER P. (1980) The British Economy in the 1970s, Hutchinson

MAYNARD, Geoffrey, (1988) The Economy under Mrs Thatcher, Basil Blackwell

MORGAN, Kenneth, (1990)The People's Peace, Oxford University Press

PARSONS, D.W. (1985) The Political Economy of British Regional Policy, Croom Helm

POLLARD, Sidney, (1985)The Development of the British Economy, 1914-1980, Edward Arnold

REES, Gareth & LAMBERT, John (1985) Cities in Crisis, Edward Arnold

Ed RICHARDSON, Jeremy & HENNING, Roger, (1984) Unemployment, Sage Publications

RIDELL, Peter, (1983) The Thatcher Government, Martin Robertson

ROBSON, Brian, (1988) Those Inner Cities, Clarendon Press

ROUTH, Guy, (1986) Unemployment and Economic Perspectives, Macmillan

SHANKS, Michael, (1977) Planning and Politics, George Allen & Unwin

SHELDRAKE, John & VICKERSTAFFE, Sarah, (1987) The History of Industrial Training in Britain, Gower Publishing

SHOWLEA, Brian, (1976) The Public Employment Service, Longman

SKED, Alan & COOK Chris, (1979) Post-War Britain, Penguin Books

SMITH, John Grieve, (1992) Full Employment in the 1990s, Institute for Public Policy Research

TAYLOR, Robert, (1980) The Fifth Estate, Pan Books

TAYLOR, Robert, (1982) Workers & The New Depression, Macmillan

THATCHER, Margaret, (1986) The Downing Street Years, Harper Collins

THERBORN, Goran, (1986) Why Some people are more Unemployed than others, Verso

WORSWICK, D.G.N. & ADY, P.H The British Economy in the 1950s, Oxford University Press

OFFICIAL PUBLICATIONS

Cmd 6404	Social Insurance & Allied Services 1942
Cmd 6527	Employment Policy, 1944
Cmd 9725	Economic Implications of Full Employment, 1956
Cmnd 1432	The Control of Public Expenditure, 1961
Cmnd 2764	The National Plan, 1965
Cmnd 3623	Report of Royal Commission on Trade Unions and Employers Associations, 1968
Cmnd 3888	In Place of Strife, 1969
Cmnd 7293	Winning the Battle Against Inflation, 1978
Cmnd 9474	Employment, The Challenge to the Nation, 1985

Ministry of Labour/Department of Employment Gazette throughout period 1945-1983.